DANDELIONS BLOOMING IN
THE CRACKS OF SIDEWALKS

To Pastor Chad,

Warmly,

Amita

(daughter Earl & Betty Tatum)

Published by Mandorla Publications
Napa, CA 94581
© 2019 by Amita Lhamo
All rights reserved

Library of Congress Control Number: 2018913704

ISBN 978-0-9980447-0-5 (pbk. : alk. Paper) –ISBN 978-0-9980447-1-2 (ebook)

1. Death-Psychological Aspects 2. Spirituality 3. Terminally Ill

First printing, January 2019
ISBN 978-0-9980447-0-5
Manufactured in USA on acid free, FSC Certified paper
Designed by Studio Carnelian
Set in Adobe Caslon
Printed and bound by McNaughton & Gunn

Mandorla Publications is the publishing imprint for The Mandorla Project,
a 501 (c) dedicated to exploring the relationship between spirituality
and care for the dying.

www.themandorlaproject.org

DANDELIONS BLOOMING *in the* CRACKS — *of* — SIDEWALKS

Stories from the Bedside of the Dying

AMITA LHAMO

Mandorla Publications

2019

For Zach

"Let come what comes. Let go what goes.
See what remains."

—*Ramana Maharshi*

Contents

Contents, *continued*

FOREWORD

MANY YEARS AGO, Amita Lhamo told me a story of entering the room of a man on the very brink of death, hallucinating and agitated.

"Do you know what is happening?" she asked.

Her question, like a lightning bolt in a storm, pierced the decades-long density of his mental illness. He died a few moments later, in the peace and clarity of prayer.

I have often recalled that story and aspired to be as clear and fearless when entering the presence of the dying.

Now Amita has offered us a diverse collection of such stories, based on her work as a hospice chaplain and, more profoundly, her inner work during years of meditation retreat. Versed in the poetry and beauty of various spiritual traditions, she accesses the most appropriate methods and words that guide those in the transition of dying to recognize the love, spaciousness and purity of their essential being. In her interactions at the bedside, she sometimes offers humor, sometimes gentle confrontation, but always she offers prayer and the flow of breath that merge with the dying person's journey.

Dandelions Blooming in the Cracks of Sidewalks: Stories from the Bedside of the Dying, is lyrical and coherent—the bedside stories connected by insights drawn from Amita's rich store of knowledge and life experience.

Reading—and re-reading—these stories feel like entering a unique series of realms, each within a sphere of compassion and total concentration on the particular needs of the person who is dying. Amita's presence invites us in. We, who would hesitate outside the door wondering what to do, will find ourselves inside, intimately included.

Within such intimacies, Amita guides us through grief-struck paralysis and helplessness in the face of pain, terminal illness and the inevitability of death into the creative possibilities of genuine companionship. Accompanying her on these end-of-life journeys, we find unexpected moments of joy. We feel a little less afraid of our own deaths as well.

In the Buddhist teachings that anchor my understanding of how one's consciousness transits dying and death, there is no higher aspiration than 'all-pervasive compassion'—vast compassion that arises from a wisdom beyond formulaic constructs to spontaneously meet the needs of others.

This book encourages us not only to offer our time, love and attention to others, but also to engage our own practices of prayer and meditation, so that we gain confidence in our own gestures of compassion, love, and joy to create benefit in the great interdependence of living and dying.

Chagdud Khadro
Chagdud Gonpa Khadro Ling
Rio Grande do Sul, Brasil

INTRODUCTION

ONE SUMMER, SOME FRIENDS and I sat around a patio table fantasizing what we might do if we could rewrite the stories of our lives. Seasoned professionals in our fields, we engaged the panoply of world problems with solutions hewn from our daily observations. We asked what we could give to an ever-changing world.

Yet, when my turn came, I fumbled with the practicalities, unable to invent a new platform, and simply said, "I'd point to the beauty."

There was an uncomfortable silence as the bantering encouragement momentarily ceased. Everyone looked at their drinks, their hands, the setting sun, until someone finally asked, "Then why are you working with death?"

I had no reply.

Years later, I gave a talk to a local spiritual fellowship, trying to summarize all I'd learned at the deathbed.

"When I looked for suffering, I found suffering," I told them. "When I looked for beauty, I found the one suffering. Together we found an ineffable presence rising through the seams of all we sought. The profundity changed us all."

I didn't expect this when I first began my work as a hospice chaplain. Like so many, I arrived with a list of burning questions, a need to heal, and just enough skills to give while I figured it all out.

I'd turned my mind toward care for the dying when, as a practicing psychotherapist, I told my first spiritual teacher, Tari, "I'm tired of cleaning up all the messes. I'm tired of talking about the past, the future…everything. Isn't it possible to be present within the halls of transformation when it is a necessity rather than another bandaid?"

"You've hit upon the limitations of psychology. What is it you really want to know?"

A few weeks later, I returned. "I've learned how the ego is put together. I want to know what happens when it comes apart."

"That is spirituality. That is death."

In college, I had taken a course on death, dying, and grief. At the time, it was only the second course taught at a university level in the country. Like our school, most felt the topic unworthy, unsuitable, even unethical, and therefore, inappropriate for college students. Few were qualified to teach, and those who were had limited contexts from which to share what they knew.

Drawn into the material, for reasons I still can't fully explain, I went on to provide counseling at the university veterinary hospital as owners grappled with terminal diagnoses for their pets, offered grief groups at the residential treatment center where I worked, became a teaching assistant for the course, and took graduate-level training when that became available as well. As a psychotherapist, I specialized in grief therapy long before it was popular.

"I think it is time for me to work with the dying," I told Tari. She simply nodded her head.

Within months, my family and I moved to a new state. Pregnant with our second child, I closed the door to my clinical practice, imagining the richness of family life in lieu of all the pain, suffering, and grief of the world.

I became sick, within a few weeks of our move, with a viral infection no one could identify. Within a month, I laid in bed full time amidst unpacked boxes, while strangers from a nearby Unitarian Universalist Fellowship quickly became friends. They cared for our son, Zach, brought food, and washed dishes while my husband, Rob, worked at his new job and I tried to heal, protecting the pregnancy as long as possible.

Regardless, the asthmatic coughing wouldn't abate, and I kept losing fluids from what we'd later learn was a tear in the placenta. One day, the bleeding required another visit to the emergency room. This time I was admitted.

It was summertime, the week of my birthday, my dearest friends now a time zone away as I lay on the maternity floor listening to other mothers birth their healthy babies. I remained as still as possible, doing everything I was told, hoping goodness would reverse symptoms just long enough for our baby to thrive. I was only 28 weeks pregnant when labor started.

We heroically tried to turn these tides with muscle relaxants that left me unable to think clearly or turn alone in the bed, as heart palpitations and fluid in my lungs threatened my health. Another ultrasound showed our baby far behind gestational markers. We were asked to decide the next step.

This time is a blur of disjointed thoughts, statistics from a medical text Rob read, the rhythmic pulse of dampened contractions, and a dream that finally turned the tide.

"Our daughter is dying. My body has been saying so for weeks." We stopped all medical intervention; the contractions briefly stopped, and I slept for the first time in nearly a week.

When nearly dilated, contractions pounding one atop another, I wept and howled as a kind nurse, who'd sat with me for two nights in a row, whispered to the nurse midwife, "Isn't there anything we can give her for the pain?"

"I am birthing a baby who is going to die. There is no medication for this!"

Maggie lived for an hour upon my naked breast. She'd gulp air, then rest, sip, silence, eyes closed, fingers wrapped around mine, toes curled against skin as we tried to keep her warm.

Time stopped. The poetry of birth unfurled into a silent wonder. Death seamlessly arose upon the current, pushing and pulling across a single threshold. We were awed by the perfection. It was nothing less than holy.

A few days later, sorrow stormed our house and my body, bringing confusion with it. I recoiled, tucking the beauty into a vault so it couldn't haunt me. I buried the creative generativities that had led us all.

"Joy and sorrow share the same piece of soil," Lama Drimed Norbu told me years later in one of our earliest meetings.

I wish I'd known that then, for the opposition of beauty and grief tore me apart, our marriage too.

Nonetheless, nine months later, I became pregnant once more after a self-inflicted boot-camp regimen of preparation. With a second loss now staining my records, as my first pregnancy, before Zach, had ended in a late miscarriage, I was shuttled to a doctor's office, which barraged my newly-gained confidence with high-tech monitoring I somehow translated as shame.

I chose to work with homebirth midwives across the mountains instead, using backup doctors who continued weekly, specialized ultrasounds, well past the point when Maggie had left the womb too early. Together, we created a holistic plan of care. Everything appeared to be fine, despite a nagging voice I attributed to anxiety and strange in-utero movements that didn't make sense until later.

As I approached the end of the pregnancy, the baby dropped into my pelvis, preparing for birth. Something didn't feel right as movements slowed from their keep-me-up-all-night vigor, but when asked, I said, "I think everything's alright." At our check-up the next day, there was no heartbeat. Our baby had died.

It took nearly five days to jumpstart labor. I'd shower, trying to ignore my belly. Avoided anyone that might ask when my baby was due. Once again, we sent Zach home with friends, as I tried to convince my body to cooperate.

One afternoon, I took a walk, through a nearby rose garden, sat down, and shouted to the sky, "Well, you very well better give me an explanation this time!"

I didn't know how to hold death and life within a single womb. This was all I knew of prayer.

The next day, doctors managed to get labor started with an off-label experimental drug, which tore my body open while I tried to ride the torrent. Floating in a birthing pool, fully dilated, I asked, "Do I have to look at my baby?"

They'd warned me that, after nearly a week, flesh might have torn apart like a corpse tossed onto a heap of soil on a hot day. There might not be a baby to look at. I was afraid to look at the destruction of death.

"No. The choice is yours."

I wept again, and with a few strong pushes birthed our son, Oliver, crying, "I changed my mind. Please don't take him away."

The doctor handed him to me, her face twisted in grief as she said, "This is why he died."

There was a perfect knot in the umbilical cord, wrapped twice around his neck. He suffocated when he dropped deep into my pelvis to prepare for birth. He would have been so small while swimming in such precise circles that even high resonant ultrasounds couldn't see the knot. He had been struggling for breath all along.

I had an answer this time. I fell to my knees, broken nonetheless.

※　※　※

When I began my work as a hospice chaplain, I'd moved to a new city. Newly divorced, I tried to start over and put it all behind me.

One winter, as I prepared a sermon for the annual Hospice ritual of recognizing the deceased, I prepared two introductions. One was personal while the other was clinical.

I'd been quite sick with a bronchial condition. So, on the evening of our event, I sat alone in my office to avoid conversations, hoping my voice would carry through all the public speaking. I still practiced both options, figuring I'd choose once I stepped up to the podium.

When I entered the room, to my surprise, nearly three hundred people were piled into our newly completed building. As I offered the invocation, I scanned the crowd. Row by row, chair by chair, I knew each family, nearly every face. I'd been to their homes, sat on their couches, stood in their bedrooms, held trembling hands—shared breath, secrets, unspoken words. I could no longer separate myself from the intimacy. I shared my story publicly for the first time.

I'd briefly trained as a homebirth midwife. Even after

Oliver's death, I was still struck by the profundity of birth, even death, and the ways midwifery embraces it all. Of all the people in my life at that time, only midwives spoke to me as a woman and a mother rather than as a failure or recalcitrant child. They included me within the cycles of life rather than exiling me as an abhorrent outlier.

Yet I could not stand up beneath the pile of blame, my own included, in which midwives and mothers were accused, even prosecuted, whenever things didn't go as planned. I still had too much fear, so I trained in spiritual care for the dying instead.

It wasn't until I began to train others to offer such care that I realized my losses were initiatory rather than punishment, neglect, or the private litany of "would have, could have, should have," I still chanted. With each workshop I taught, one, perhaps two or three people would come forward with a sincere desire to sit with the dying. Within hours, a week, a month or two, death would visit their house with a regularity that made me pause and reexamine my motives for teaching. They reeled with the demands of death as I once did.

We cannot avoid death, but we can gaze deeply into its eyes, ask our questions, and walk with one another. This, of course, is what we're most afraid of. To dance with death sheers away all the good ideas, rips off scabs and masks, unties all our neatly packaged stories and impermanent defenses, and leaves us naked with the rest of humanity, with all sentient life.

This is also the beauty. We cannot escape. Death surges through the very center of our being, tearing off all the fig leaves. We can comfort the pain, the anxiety, the suffering. We can also gaze through the cracking shells to see what else lives in such places. What shines through the brokenness? What remains?

To look for the beauty is to recognize that we are not our

suffering. Within the intimacy of kindness, we learn to stay just long enough to grow minds that can hold the paradox of living and dying simultaneously. No matter which way we turn, we find one garden, one ground.

Each soul is a wondrous flower. To gaze into the face of any one of us is to see it all. *Namaste*—the God in me sees the God in you.

Perhaps this is why we need stories. We look for a language that can invite us into the invisible landscapes with the courage of one who's gone before. We find our place within the necessity of a path only we can walk.

Each of us carries stories about ourselves, our world, life and death, that knowingly or unknowingly guide each step, each decision, each emotional reaction. They are forged from memory, experience, even lack of experience—tools meant to engage the known and the unknown alike.

Historically, one role of religion has been to turn our minds from the limitations of these personal stories by offering a "meta-narrative," stories about reality that can shave away cyclic habits and cataractic views, and place us within a more uplifting interpretation of reality instead. It is the first step for transcending all narratives, good or bad, that we may experience ourselves as flowers in the ground of being, free of all prescriptive glasses.[1]

The difficulty in our current era, most especially for Westerners, is a love-hate relationship with the teaching stories of our ancestry. Nearly every poll finds that, as a whole, we believe in Divine forces, even God, yet fewer and fewer attend any formalized ritual, gathering, or regular services.[2] We are rejecting the stories that once guided us, and with their dismissal, we stand face to face with the forces of life and death, relying upon entertainment and media networks to guide us instead.[3] We ask modern healers to be shamans. We steal stories from other cultures and then cut and paste them upon Western minds still forged in the fires of our own history. We reify stories that no longer serve, arguing with evidence to the contrary, narrowing the stories themselves to serve personal motivations.

This is an especially pronounced issue when it comes to death. Not only did we remove the myths that guide both our belief systems, as well as our psychological engagement, we simultaneously removed ourselves from death, placed it in the remote hands of experts, and, in doing so, misplaced the wisdom born from personal, familial, and communal experience.

The average person has never seen someone die. Yet death is forever in our living rooms, on televisions and computer screens, in magazines and newspapers, as common as the weather report. It's a noise like traffic we sit through, but lacking any personal context unless the hurricane strikes our neighborhood.

Our lack of experience and our hunger for news creates a milieu of tragedy, an expectation of pain. So much of what we talk about, even decide, is born from the conjecture of ideas meant to assuage our fears rather than engage death directly. We enter this stage of our lives without any maps, dissociating all we've learned about spirituality from the dying process.

Yet something different happens when we invite death into the conversation. It enters amidst a panoply of experience that includes gratitude, love, joy, and wonder. Within this milieu, we learn an intimacy that acknowledges the entirety of the human experience. We open rather than fight or run. Within such spaces, souls peek through all the hope and fear like dandelions blooming in the cracks of sidewalks. We find beauty within the humble contours of our lives.

Joseph Campbell taught that story or myth has four primary functions.[4]

The first is to reconcile the conditions of our existence through the balm of gratitude, love, and a deep recognition of the core sweetness of life. We affirm our place within the evolution of creation, whether we reject the world or accept it, whether life turned out as we planned or darted through unexpected pastures. We bow with gratitude and awe before the wonder of existence.

The second is to offer a view of the universe, the cosmos, that engenders this gratitude or awe. We learn how to enter a field of play within which we reconcile our lives, our conscious interiors, and find meaning. It could be unproven, unprovable, scientifically false, lack all consensual agreement, yet behave as a truth through which we can maintain contact with wonder, curiosity, and even awe in a way that makes sense and keeps us going back for more.

The third function validates and maintains what most of us would call ethics, the means with which we protect the life we all share. We teach ourselves how to live with one another—what is fair, what is helpful, what is kind, what sustains, and what threatens. We unfurl and develop personal values within an ethos that includes everyone, regardless of differences.

Finally, mythology serves our psychological development, guiding us through each stage of life from birth through death. We learn how to enter our own interiors while simultaneously engaging the exterior, the world around us. We dance upon the invisible barrier between us, one molding the other, until this too dissolves.

Yet "the best things can't be told—they are transcendent, inexpressible truths."[5] Myths or stories point toward this too, inviting us into the places we can know for ourselves if we can only suspend our disbelief, our need to understand, perhaps even our desire to control, just long enough to traverse the landscape. Stories are koans, both upending and leading us.

This is why I began teaching about death through stories.

As a culture, the first thing we did when we finally re-opened Pandora's box of death was jump to our lists of what to do. We put everything into categories and implemented our plans accordingly. We focused much of our efforts on the outer forms of intervention, expectation, and preferential outcomes without exploring the role of death in our lives. We believed healing existed within the capacity to eliminate symptoms rather than the interior transformation of any one of us. We separated healing from the processes of dying. We separated the living from the dying.

Yet at the heart of midwifery one human being sits with another. The word midwife translates as, "Be with...be with woman." Together we explore malleable truths through the labyrinth of any heart. We lead and follow, follow and lead, and within the dialogue, we become present to presence.

This book is a collection of such stories, gleaned from thousands of conversations around the deathbed. Each one reflects a quality of beauty, of soulness—the ways any one of us reflects the profundity of existence.

"Beauty is the harvest of presence," wrote David Whyte. "The evanescent moment of seeing or hearing on the outside what already lives far inside us."[6]

Before death, our greatest strengths and vulnerabilities arise. We grapple with every hope and fear imaginable. It is my wish that these stories can offer wisdom, reassurance, solace, encouragement, and confidence for anyone standing before the mirror of finitude. Perhaps they can offer guidance while we remember what already lives within. Perhaps they can point to the presence of beauty.

Not every story is easy. We cannot underestimate the torrent of death. We simply learn to find ourselves within the spaces through which all currents run, including death. This makes room for everything else.

There are many ways to approach these stories. They can be read all at once, or one at a time as a means for contemplation. In the same way, they can be approached privately or shared aloud with friends.

Each one stands alone as part of a collection. Together, they speak to the qualities of beauty and some of the ways we see, lean into, and experience it. They connect some of what we know about spirituality to dying. They offer familiar ways we can love one another. They invite us into our own minds and hearts, to taste this beauty for ourselves, to know beauty within. They invite us into the ineffable nature of awareness.

As I wrote this book, I felt into the living memories of all the men and women I once sat with—the ways we had touched one another. These are not stories of the mythological other, but of fellow pilgrims walking the same trail we do. In this light, no matter what you may seek in these pages, what motivates you to read them, please remember that these stories were the final gifts of precious beings, who both gazed into the bowels of death and shared the journey. Their beauty arose within the profundity of their humanness.

For around the deathbed, when all the reconciliations, confessions, ideations, and activities release, the soul smiles, leaving a scent, a song, a vision, a silent wisdom as it fades into the sky like a shooting star. None of us can claim such bounty.

We simply behold the wonder, weave it into the abundance of our own lives, and give it away—again, and again, and again.

HOSPITALITY

The root word for hospice originated in Biblical times when safe houses were established for travelers needing shelter from weather and bandits.[7] Sharing the same etymology as hospital and hotel, the Latin derivative, hospis, *points to both the host and guest, inferring an interdependent relationship.[8]*

Historically, strangers found refuge in the kindness of those willing to share food, wine, and housing as they traveled. Whether war or famine drove them from their home, or the spiritual imperative of pilgrimage called them forth, their survival depended upon the kindness of others.

Healers, midwives, shamans, teachers, and bards also traveled between villages, offering their gifts. They shared the same road, and when night came, they too, sought food, drink, housing, and even health care.

One could never be sure who might be knocking at their door. The ethics of hospitality ensured that strangers were greeted with kindness.

I've always loved the tradition of midwives leaving their homes in the middle of the night to help babies enter and elders pass on. It feels natural to leave my personal world behind and enter the world of another.

Within the thinning veils, we share a path that moves beyond our ordinary eyes, linking us across the sacred spaces we all must travel. Home becomes a sanctuary, an altar for the generations of becoming.

To arrive as a guest dissolves the hierarchies, opens the mind to a shared experience, and in doing so, broadens our view.

Perhaps this is part of the hospice success story. The dying rest within the refuge of familiar surroundings, and we begin our care with the humility of knocking.

For a little while, the dying become the center of attention. We enter their home and give from the heart of a traveler, our expertise born from the journey.

Yet, as a provider of spiritual care, it hasn't always been easy to receive the invitation necessary to enter a home. We don't usually look like pilgrims or even teachers when we knock. Rather, we take the shape and size of someone's experience with religion, spiritual leaders, or their own inner worlds.

Spirituality is an elusive term, defined more by what it isn't than what it is, for it is the unique way that wisdom and compassion emerge within the vast space of any heart.

We can talk about this indefinitely, but until we know this within our own hearts, it is an idea that will die with all the rest. We cannot enter this sacred space with another concept or expectation, not even a good one. This is true of someone's home as well.

The husband of a friend who died, after two years of weekly phone calls and home visits, said a few weeks after her death, "I couldn't have known what you do until I experienced it."

"That's okay. I can't know what I do until I give it."

The true test of a master comes when the path requires a teacher to shed dependency upon form, and act within the moment rather than from tradition alone. We leave our identifications, credentials, and resumes at the door and embrace a trust born within the naked intention of love.

We simply start giving.

※　※　※

ONE MORNING, I NOTICED a few nurses huddled in whispers, two of them crying, as they discussed how to offer medical care to a family that requested our presence and a patient who refused all care.

Claude had been discharged from the hospital when no other curative options remained. Cancer had devoured his mouth, jaw, muscle, and skin. He breathed through a trachea tube, unable to speak. His face was swollen and raw from festering wounds. He was no longer recognizable as the man he once was.

To make matters worse, each night Claude would try to crawl up the stairs to where his family slept. Unfortunately he didn't have the strength, and more times than not, would fall, adding additional cuts and bruises to his medical needs. Then he would strike out at anyone who tried to help him back to bed. They'd yell and argue until the family gave up and returned to bed, leaving Claude to sleep on the stairs. He'd return to his bed in the living room the next morning, and the cycle would repeat. Everyone hurt.

As the nurses searched for ways to navigate the layers of difficulty, I felt inspired by their willingness to seek kindness rather than recoil or judge. They saw what the cancer and chaos made others forget. I wanted to support their efforts and asked if I could come along, not to see the patient but to support the nurse.

"I just want to come and silently pray, be a familiar and supportive face for the nurse to rely upon."

The nurse taking the case didn't want to break down in front of the family. She welcomed the support. Thanks to encouragement by both the nurse and the social worker, Claude's wife received me the next day.

It was Christmas time, so when I came to the door, she greeted me with cookies and coffee, which it turned out I couldn't refuse, for to do so wasn't merely impolite, it broke the rules of cultural etiquette.

"Americans just don't get it," she announced. "One does not refuse food when it's offered. The recipe for these cookies was given from my great-grandmother to my grandmother to my mother to me. We don't give them to strangers. Look, I've brought you the best batch. Aren't you hungry?"

I started drinking the strongest coffee I'd ever tasted, hoping my tea-drinking ways could handle the sudden surge of sugar and caffeine.

She and Claude had emigrated from Eastern Europe some thirty years before. Between bites, she told the story of their travels, the conditions that brought them to the States, the similarities and differences, the Christmas traditions they still kept. She flipped through several photo albums strewn across the table, pointing to a photo of visiting family on their first trip to the States. They posed in front of the church they attended twice a year on Christmas and Easter. She hadn't called the priest yet, though she would ask him to perform the funeral because "there's nothing he can do anyway. In our country, we'd make my husband take the medicine."

I noticed a small deck of cards with an angel on the top tucked behind a magazine, and when I asked, learned they were a tarot deck of angels in which you pick a card to see what blessing or energy one needed, what prayer could be uttered. I asked if we could play, and she sheepishly pulled them out, leading me to believe she didn't think chaplains would partake in such games, and I wondered if she ever had either.

She pulled the card Gabriel—the angel that announced to Mother Mary her impending pregnancy with the Christ child. Then she relayed a story her mother once told her after a bad dream.

"Gabriel watches over us, whispering secrets, preparing us for all life brings. The news isn't always good, but listening to him makes the journey easier. He can see much more than we can." She let out a deep sigh.

"Do you think this is true?" she asked.

"I think all sorts of things we don't understand are true. What is Gabriel saying to you?"

Tearing up she said, "I'm going to be a widow. I've never lived alone before. I hope I'll be alright."

We talked about Claude, who'd ruled their house like an angry king, which to her said more about leadership than character. He could always be counted upon to forge through, to drag everyone behind him, even if they resisted, including a move halfway around the world. He'd taught her how to make a new home among strangers when she wanted to quit. She relied upon him despite their frequent arguments.

The man in the other room no longer looked stubborn, victimized, or even angry. He looked proud, courageous, his tenacity a sign of love for his family, a story we didn't understand yet.

"Could I return with the nurse tomorrow? Offer silent prayers for you and your family while she cares for your husband?"

"Oh, yes. I'll bake cookies."

She welcomed us the next day, and after our initial greetings, I sat in the dining room with my cup of coffee and plate of Christmas cookies while the nurse quietly entered the living room where the patient crouched in the corner of a sofa bed. Fortunately, the doorway from the dining room looked through the kitchen, which opened up into the living room. The nurse and I could see each other continuously.

His family and I talked for a little while, but then I reminded them that I'd come to pray and asked for their support, which they immediately offered. They busied themselves in the kitchen, talking, sometimes disagreeing, while the nurse, bit by bit, cleaned facial wounds and his tracheotomy for the next two hours.

She never forced Claude to do anything, patiently waiting for him to catch his breath before cleaning another section, pausing again as he held his forehead to manage the pain, then continuing. She'd offer him pain medication, and when he refused, didn't offer it again, telling him he could change his mind at any time. She'd look at me, and I would nod or smile, and return to prayer.

We did this for several weeks, spending at least three afternoons a week in the same ritual of prayer, patience, and kindness.

Then one day Claude whispered to the nurse, "Who comes with you?"

None of us had mentioned anything about my visits as we were afraid Claude might ban me from the premises. She simply told him the truth—that I came with her each visit to pray, then asked if he'd like me to pray with him. Claude nodded yes, surprising us all.

I slipped in quietly and sat down across from him without speaking anything more than, "Hello."

I looked deeply into his face, past the swelling around both eyes, the crusts and scabs now acting like skin, the spittle draining from lips he couldn't close—the suffering that had become his life. I never felt a need to turn away, though I often prepared myself for what I'd do if I did.

His breath betrayed the effort required for him to return the gaze. A muffled sound, like the determined whimper of a beaten child, caught the edge of each rise and fall. Yet I also heard a wind, like a gale passing across the mouth of a cave that drew me through the storm to a hidden shelter. I paused there. Claude did too.

Somehow, this was all either of us needed to know, for he turned back to the nurse, who continued her work, without dismissing me as we'd all once expected. When she asked me to help her change the sheets, I did, and he didn't fight either of us.

With each subsequent visit, I simply sat on the couch in silent prayer, though sometimes, we'd begin and end holding hands. I'd gaze into Claude's eyes, and he into mine.

Then the nurse would return to her work, and I'd return to the couch. Periodically, Claude would check to see if I was still present, the way Zach would look for me on the side of the pool when he first learned to swim alone with friends. I'd pray with my eyes open, meditating really, watching, as though nothing else existed but this.

Soon, each time we entered, everyone in the house became quiet, and the family began to participate too, bringing a clean shirt or pillowcase, a vase of flowers. The cookies and coffee stopped, as did the conversations. Sometimes, his wife would sit with me, take my hand, and we'd also breathe together.

One day we arrived to find Claude sleeping, his head on the pillow, his body unfurled from weeks of fighting from his corner. Clean sheets and blankets were tucked around him. He'd said yes to pain medication and was finally resting.

On the last day of his life, the nurse cleaned his wounds for a few minutes, then returned the instruments to her bag, saying, "No more. It's time to pray."

Claude sat up and scooted to the edge of the bed. I knelt before him as he laid his head on the nurse's shoulder while she held him. Then he wrapped his arm around my knees as his family joined us. Suddenly, Claude looked up at the ceiling and gasped.

"Do you know what's happening?" I asked him. The first words I'd ever spoken to him.

He nodded and leaned toward me, only a few inches away, as I whispered, "On your own time. Each breath your guide. You are not alone."

We gazed deeply into one another's eyes for the last time. Claude laid his cheek upon the nurse's hand as though to offer her a kiss. Then, we tucked him back into bed. His family crawled in beside him.

They were lying together in silence as he took his final breaths.

TRUE NATURE

One afternoon, Tari said, "Do not leave your first meeting with some-one until you've shown them who they really are. This is the healing. Give them a taste of their true nature."

I'd recounted a particularly complicated situation in which few solutions were available. I felt helpless.

"The healing comes not in answers but knowing that someone can create an answer, and that this someone exists within."

So I ventured back to my office, wondering how to show someone her true self.

One day, a long-term client and I spent an hour talking about our relationship. She'd recently returned from the hospital, both of us rattled by her brush with death.

We met to discuss all we'd learned in the previous months, and the road ahead. As we processed all the qualities of self she discovered, I said, "You're becoming."

"Becoming what?" she chuckled.

"All of this, none of this, and more."

We shared a welcome moment of levity.

At the end of our time, I turned to my desk to write her a receipt. When I swiveled back she had receded into a gold sphere, as if con-sumed by alchemical light. Her face appeared like a luminous dream, her body floating within the radiance. I blinked, and blinked again, beholding what I could only call an angel.

As I contemplated her transformation, I realized that she'd taught me more about the psyche than all the years of my academic career, as though she were the one bestowing the gifts. Overwhelmed by gratitude, I knew I would offer anything I could to help her.

To see her as an angel, rather than broken, offered her the opportunity to see this too. After two years, the struggles leading to her suicide attempt simply stopped.

❊   ❊   ❊

WHEN A YOUNG MAN IN HIS FIFTIES managed to pull through his latest hospital stay, after a bout of drinking that had exacerbated his end-stage liver disease, he uncharacteristically received visits from everyone after his near miss.

The sudden influx of people still did very little to touch his depression. He remained listless on the couch, even as his symptoms subsided, and refused food, self-care, anything that could be called life affirming. Despair permeated everything.

"What are you doing here?" he asked me.

"I'm not really sure."

"I thought you types had an agenda. You can't convert me you know."

"That's kind of a relief."

"Really?"

"Yeah, that'd be a lot of pressure. What if I picked the wrong spell and you became a rabbit? Your life doesn't belong in my hands."

Then we were quiet, except for a little small talk now and again, as I wondered what I was doing there, thinking it was the most relevant question on the table, when he said, "You know, when I die, it's all over. I'm dead and that's that."

"Yes, dead is dead."

He smiled.

"I mean, you could just throw my body out there," he said, glancing toward the window, "and it wouldn't even matter, because I'd be dead. It'd all be over."

"Hmmm… well, I don't know if it matters or not, but it isn't really over." He looked at me with a here-it-comes look.

"I'm not exactly sure what happens to you, whether you would notice your corpse in the garden or not. But I do know that you can't destroy atoms, although you can make a pretty deadly bomb trying.

"Your corpse out there would simply reconfigure itself. All the atoms that bond together to make what we call you would come apart, and then each atom would re-bond to other atoms, repeating this enough times until something new was made.

"Nothing really dies on a cellular level. It just keeps morphing. So from this perspective, dead isn't really dead. It's just change."

He became quite still, stared out the window so long I thought he'd end our conversation, when he asked, "Did anyone tell you what I studied in college?"

"No."

"Double major in physics and mathematics."

"Oh," I swallowed.

He laughed.

"Am I telling the truth, or should I get out some paper and take a physics lesson?"

"Yes," he said. "What you say is true."

He invited me to visit again.

The next week he cut straight to the chase, "Do you think I could become a flower? I mean, if they threw my corpse out there, do you think I could improve my lot and become a flower?"

"I think anything's possible, but maybe we better do something with the soil. That hill's covered in weeds."

With the support of a volunteer who helped him till the land, a nurse and home health aide who gently persuaded him to receive their help, and a social worker who could coax feelings to the surface, he was outside in the garden, weeding and sowing seeds within a month.

He lived for three more years, believing he might become a flower.

IT'S A WONDERFUL LIFE

For those of us engaged in this work, there is always one client, sometimes two, that changes us indelibly. We meet at those inevitable crossroads like weft and warp, inviting one another into the necessities of change.

Tom and I met when a close friend of his heard me speak about spiritual pain. Already in hospice, he only allowed visits from the nurse until his friend convinced him that he might have spiritual pain and asked him to see me.

Perhaps it was a common view, the sacred land where he and his partner lived, our similarity in age, or the frequent laughter, but we connected and delved into recesses of the heart I'd only heard about but not yet seen.

I cannot say who led whom in these places, only that we entered together. We plumbed the depths of the spiritual path in a way that was so human it stripped common practices to their essence.

A few days before he died, I wept at my desk in anticipation of his death. A fellow chaplain checked on me, and I did my best to express not only my feelings but the depth of all that Tom and I had shared.

When I said it would take some time for me figure it all out, he replied, "You need to teach this."

"I'm not a good enough person!" I blurted, confessing mistakes, pain, and regret as he patiently listened.

When I finished, he simply replied, "Well, then you need to become a better person, because we need to know about what you're doing." I could only nod and cry.

I spent the next few weeks contemplating the potency of Tom's death and the strange comfort my friend offered. I reeled before the possibility of teaching, from both fear and respect. I still didn't understand everything that had happened, and didn't feel like I could share his story, or the practices we shared until I did. I decided that I would not teach without further training.

A few months after I made this promise, I met a new friend. When I told her about Tom, all the questions our relationship evoked, and the deep sense of responsibility I felt both toward him and the spiritual path, she introduced me to a lineage of practitioners and teachers directly connected to the practices we used.

I began by taking a weekend workshop, which naturally led to another, until I met the teacher who would guide me into the heart of all my questions. I wrote this book following a five-year meditation retreat in which I finally kept the commitments I whispered that rainy afternoon.

Although I can point to a great many factors leading me to this place, I can safely say that my relationship with Tom was a seed that changed the course of my life. In our last conversation, Tom said something similar about the impact of our time together upon his death.

If we examine the contours of any life, we'll find that our wounds and talents share the same corridors. Need and gift rub against one another like waves upon beach glass. We find each other in the surf— teaching, leading, following, encouraging, giving, and receiving.

Our lives are a tapestry of the entire play.

❋ ❋ ❋

OUR FIRST MEETING felt like a clever poker game, each of us surveying the other for some gesture that would reveal secrets. We eased our way into the conversation, quickly exchanging quips and jokes. Their dog darted in and out, sniffing and licking my shoes, rendering his own opinion.

With the pleasantries finished, Tom tentatively shared the death of their previous dog, whose photo held a place of honor on a nearby table.

After their dog died, he and his partner, Richard, had flown his body to Arizona and met with a medicine man and friend, who, after a dream ceremony, led them to the chosen burial site and offered ritual. They'd seen many signs—a circling hawk, a dancing cloud—he'd even had a vision.

As he shared the story of his dog, it seemed he was trying to tell me what he sought, as he wove himself into a narrative that included death. He became still, his words careful, as he recalled the season, the color of the sky, the heat, the distant mountains, his beating heart. When he finished, neither of us spoke. We simply stared out the window across the manicured hills and the wild forest just beyond.

"Do you see that?" Tom asked. "Next to the willow tree?"

Coiled atop an ambling root, its head erect as if to catch a scent on the wind, a rattlesnake, at least four if not five inches in diameter and several feet long, peered directly at us.

"That's some medicine you brought with you," Tom said.

"How do you know it's mine?"

"That's where I want them to scatter my ashes," he said, still watching the snake through the window.

We paused again.

"How about the spot where the snake sits?" I asked.

"Yes, there." Tom stared back at me, or through me, then laughed and said, "You can come back."

"The rattlesnake too?"

They sent their dog to escort me back to my car. It was the middle of January. Most snakes were hibernating.

We visited every week after that, each of us telling stories, asking questions, and poking fun at everything that became too serious. He was dying of prostate cancer, bedridden, with tubes controlling most of the fluids below his waist. As the months unfolded, the lingering wait began to feel like the eve of battle, only no one could name the war.

Late that spring, I received a call when he was admitted into the hospital on the verge of palliative surgery. One of his tubes was leaking waste into a deepening wound, and the symptoms had become unmanageable. Richard felt pushed into making decisions he had no experience to handle; the fear of causing harm was a persistent pressure. He asked if I could offer anything to relieve Tom's pain since nothing else was working.

Tom lay rigid, contracted from the effort of trying to outrun the storm. Eyes darting wild, he clutched the rail on both sides of his bed, even after hours of IV medication. Richard cleared the room, and we silently breathed together.

"I have to make a decision, so no one else has to," Tom began.

"Hmmm."

"If I have the surgery, I could die on the table. It feels so cold. I can't do that to Richard. But if I go home like this, my mother will have to watch me suffer. I can't do that to her either."

"Death or suffering. Guaranteed to hurt everyone you love. Doesn't sound like much of a choice," I replied.

He laughed.

"Let's just welcome the pain, okay? Let it be here first. Love it like you would a precious child."

Then, in non-nursing terms, I asked him where the pain resided in his body.

He pointed toward his chest.

"They didn't give you a heart catheter did they?"

He laughed again, sighed, and relaxed a little more.

"Just breathe into the pain and offer it all it needs. What does your pain ask for?" I asked.

"I cannot make choices for everyone else. I need a little time, that's all."

"How much time do the doctors need before you render a decision? Are they making choices based upon your pain level or upon a crisis of symptoms?"

"I'm not sure," he replied. "I just need some quiet time. Do you think everyone could leave for a little while, so I can find myself in this?"

"All I can do is ask," and agreed to inquire on his behalf.

Then I chanted for a little while, pouring sacred words into the open wound of his heart.

His family only wanted the best for him, and with this small meditation his pain levels dropped from excruciating to manageable. Tom was clearly in control of himself again, resting quietly. They entrusted him to his privacy.

Soon afterwards, as his family left for dinner, a new nurse, fresh on the case with the change of shift, found a way to stop the leak by rigging something like a plumbing device, a technique she learned as an army nurse abroad. He no longer needed surgery, resolving the dilemma.

"An angel came last night," he said when I checked on him the next day.

"They usually just need enough space to fly," I replied.

We went through a few more pain crises, although they never took him back to the hospital. His body continued to deteriorate, though his mind stayed intact to the end. A young man, most of his body seemed oblivious to the cancer, intent on living into the future Tom once imagined.

One day, the nurse relayed that they were running out of pain management options. Tom had clearly stated his desire to stay alert to the end, but a deep wound had tunneled into his spine, eating away thinning tissues, baring his nerves to the air. The medications couldn't touch the ensuing pain with the current dosage. She felt that they might need to sedate him in order to keep him comfortable.

We visited together the next day. I held his hand as the nurse changed the dressings. When he began to yell expletives, I returned the favor, looking for all those ways we made each other laugh in the face of the impossible.

"Never done that with a chaplain before."

"How many chaplains do you know, anyhow?"

We laughed again.

"I'm human. And so are you. This is where we'll find our miracles."

Once she finished giving Tom all his prescribed medicines, the nurse left so that we could do the pain work we'd done for months.

I slipped into the dream of his breath, his body, his mind, and listened for the story trying to surface.

"Just welcome the pain, Tom. See if you can find its hiding place. The roots. The message."

To me he looked like new wine in an old wine skin, a man the size of the room stuffed into a sack splitting at the seams from the effort.

"I don't think my spirit fits anymore," he offered, as once more we traversed the same vision. With this realization, the pain immediately shot down his leg, until it channeled into a singular cramp in his foot. I gently offered healing touch, blowing prayer onto his skin with each breath. He exhaled with me and silently began to weep.

"I didn't give anything," he suddenly blurted. "I'm not important. Everything I ever did around here can be hired out to the first name in the yellow pages. Plumbing, gardening, watching the weather reports—anybody can do that. I didn't do anything important."

Tom wept as I continued to catch all the pain from the bottom of his foot.

All of a sudden he exclaimed, "It's gone. My pain is gone."

Silence.

Then he stared through me the way he had that first day. "I need to leave this body. Will you show me how? I can leave just like the pain. Tell me how."

I pondered the question for a little while as he told me more about how he'd come to live in these hills, never aspiring to a career like everyone else—what part he felt he had played.

Then, in a moment of compassion, he confessed that he'd hidden all the directions to the sprinkler systems, the electrical wiring boxes, and the land maps behind secret codes on his computer. He hadn't told anyone how to access them.

"I was afraid if I told them how to fix things, they wouldn't have a reason to visit."

He honestly believed they only visited him for instructions rather than love.

I told him a shamanic version of the film, *It's a Wonderful Life*.

"We cannot touch a leaf without affecting the entire tree. Your life matters. It always has."

"Please, help me die."

Tom didn't request doctor-assisted suicide, nor did he ask for ways to stop the pain. Rather, he explored the more subtle possibility of following and, perhaps, even guiding his own soul. He was the first to ask me so directly.

I sifted through our months of conversation, wondering how capable he would be of the kind of prayer and meditation his request demanded. I worried I wouldn't be able to advise him properly as this would be a virginal teaching built upon personal spiritual practice and classes rather than any direct experience with patients.

I simply told him the truth—what I knew and what I didn't.

"This practice has been around for about 1,500 years, and some pretty enlightened folks have been teaching it. Perhaps, we could trust this rather than our inexperience."

"Teach me," he said.

I taught him a meditation for releasing consciousness in which we enter the current of death and dive into the heart of all we seek.

Despite his lack of meditation background, he settled into the practice quickly and easily. His breath steadied, slowed, calmed. All stirring of movement stopped, all twitches, even his blinking as he lay in perfect stillness with no sign of pain. He looked asleep except for his open eyes. After an hour, I said goodbye and left him to the privacy of his meditation.

The next morning, I learned that he hadn't awoken from his meditative state the rest of that day or night, hadn't asked for pain medicines, cried out, or even stirred from his place of rest. Richard kept vigil, thinking he might die. That afternoon, they said goodbye. He wrote down all the hidden codes to his computer.

The next day, I returned with the nurse as she once more changed the dressing on his wounds. We held hands, but this time gazed into the meditation of one another's eyes—no curse words, no words of any kind. I touched his face and told him how much I loved him, and once more we returned to meditation.

I taught his partner, who taught the friends now sitting vigil, so all of us could support his practice.

This time he didn't wake up.

I visited the next day. He was in a coma, his eyes still open, with few if any differences between coma and meditative repose. Yet, this time, something moved behind his eyes, a shift behind the veil of flesh, like a ripple on still water. I felt watched by eyes that no longer needed eyes.

If I moved to the left or to the right, he imperceptibly tracked me, and when I engaged the sensation, could almost hear an invitation to play. I joined him, for there was a lightness, a quip, a laugh in the face of danger, a characteristic so unique to his soul that I recognized him anew. He played, even as a wind surged through him, around him, spiraling and traversing upward like a tornado about to leap from the ground. He sat within the heart of power and delight. Sometimes, I felt Tom. Sometimes, I felt him dissolve. Regardless, I could feel it within my own heart as if we played in the very same sky.

The next day, I was out of town when a hawk swept past me on the porch. Simultaneously, my cell phone rang. Tom had passed without any signs of struggle or pain. Richard put me on speakerphone, and I prayed aloud to all who'd gathered in those final hours, each word imbued with a wonderment that could only be named as awe. For this humble, outrageous, irreverent man had navigated and mastered the ancient art of walking into death intentionally and consciously.

A week later we held a memorial service next to the willow tree. The warmth of summer still lingered, though the leaves reminded us that winter would come soon enough. Dogs chased one another as a couple of vultures circled overhead, and a single white swan swam on the lake, but this time the snakes stayed home.

LOOK FOR THE BEAUTY

A friend once accused me of wearing rose-colored glasses. "You should have been a painter. The world you speak of doesn't exist."

It's a bit of a phenomenological dilemma, for as Hildegard de Bingen wrote, "What I do not see, I do not know."[9]

Perhaps truth is like a mandala that grows and grows with each new opening of the heart-mind.[10] The paradox, of course, is that the world can only become bigger in relationship to what we release.

A teacher in college once asked us to write down something simple about ourselves we wished we could change, like...I wish I didn't wear glasses, could lose five pounds, didn't have freckles, had black hair instead of blond, or a few more friends. We folded the paper up and passed it to the person next to us. Then, without reading it, we had to choose whether we'd release our issue in favor of a new one or take our issue back. With the exception of two people, the class of more than 100 chose to keep their own dilemma.

"We'd rather grapple with our own pain than risk the unknown," she taught.

When death arrives, it chips away at all the big and little familiarities of our lives. Bit by bit, we are stripped to the marrow of our own existence. We can feel the force, the torrent, the power, as well as our own smallness, fragility, temporality—all the uncertainty. We recognize the impenetrability of death. It can feel terrifying.

Yet Neil Douglas-Klotz teaches that beauty arises too, shining through the catalytic tremors of release. We can also taste joy, communion, even "feelings of intimacy," a resurrection from all that cannot last, a connection to all that does.[11]

From a Sufi view, these forces of power and beauty exemplify the great dance of Oneness. Change rips across the luminous sky of being like lightning, like shooting stars.

The soul, or consciousness, buries a foot in both the ephemerality and the constancy. We embody both the evolution and the ever-present presence.

Around the deathbed, our search for beauty greets the imperviousness of death with an enlarged view, teaching us to gaze, even into suffering, with innocent eyes, to see what else resides in such places.

Sometimes, it's as simple as seeing what's been there all along. Perhaps we go walking and a spout of water leaps from the sea, and we see an Orca whale for the very first time.

Sometimes, someone shows us the beauty they see, like when my son, his girlfriend, and I walk through a nearby bog. He scoops frogs into his hand, while I find all the fairy slipper orchids, and Ari studies the Bufflehead ducks. Together we learn about the landscape.

Sometimes, it's an intentional turning of the mind. We seek it. Gaze directly into what frightens us, repels us, until beauty reveals itself within the simplicity of all our questions.

❈   ❈   ❈

A NEWLY HIRED CHAPLAIN and I visited a patient who had recently been moved home after a stroke left him in an untreatable coma. Newly retired, he and his wife had planned for everything but this. We visited together so I could teach her new skills for supporting patients in comas. Neither of us had met the family before.

After all the pleasantries, we were led to a small room overlooking a rose garden. A hospital bed filled the entire space except for a small, white metal daybed tucked against the wall. We sat on the quilt-covered cushions; only two feet separated us from him as he steadily breathed without machines, defying all expectations.

We silently observed the movements of his chest as the nurse entered with his wife to clean his breathing tube. They invited us to stay, thinking it would only take a few minutes.

Suddenly, he choked. The nurse stepped between the daybed and the hospital bed to offer urgent care. We drew our legs onto the cushions to give the nurse maximum space, for we had no way to leave as he gasped for air.

His body shook as if he were having a seizure. His eyes flew open. The nurse moved quickly to open his airway. As fluids spewed, my colleague began taking short breaths, averting her eyes, and covering her mouth as if to hold back a gag reflex.

Without thinking, I commanded, "Look for the beauty! Now! Nothing else! Look for the beauty!"

She turned her mind and focused, watching the entire scene without flinching again.

Back at the office, I asked about her experience.

"What did you see?"

"His wife really loves him. I've never seen such unconditional love as that."

She described the serenity of his wife's face, her loving smile, her caressing touch, the softness of her voice each time she whispered, "It'll be alright, honey. It'll be alright."

"She's living the marriage vows. She's showing us how to love."

She had no memory of the physical complications, medical

procedures, or urgency of care. Only the beauty, now etched upon her face as well.

TRUST

There's an old adage in the midwifery community that says, "We birth the way we live." Around the deathbed we say, "We die the way we live."

The ways we engage our feelings, wishes, and beliefs, as well as our relationships, questions, and challenges, mold the means with which we face death. We tend to do what we know, following the worn paths of our habits.

Yet this phrase also points toward all the ways we've faced the unknown. All the times the familiar slipped through our fingers, and we had to call upon something deeper than tired trajectories.

This is why so many sages point to death as an opportunity, for our inability to escape shines an unyielding light upon our lives. We can see them anew and respond within the paradoxical freedom of having nothing left to lose.

Over the years, I've learned to trust this about death, and in doing so, turned toward the capacities we each carry to face the inevitabilities. It's as if death does some of the work for us, dragging us into the proverbial therapist's office to reexamine our lives against our greatest values.

We might begin by reviewing our lives—all we've been through—but eventually, we will sift through history to find the essential questions and personal expressions that continue to lead us.

A minister friend once said, "We really only have one sermon.

Each week, we explore another facet as if staring into a fluid crystal. It might take ten, twenty, thirty years, even an entire lifetime to catch the theme, the glue that holds all our questions together. We have to let it bounce around in the surf long enough to have the clarity to see into the heart of our search."

Perhaps it's enough to know that deep within us we've been chewing on wonderment, need, and intention as it pulls us through every mistake, hardship, and accomplishment, revealing not merely our gifts but also who or what has been giving. We lean into the shy innocence of our own becoming and trust the unfolding, even in death.

※　※　※

One morning, a social worker said, "I have someone I'd like you to meet."

She shared a few details.

"I didn't think he wanted to see someone like me."

"I might have slipped him a few stories."

"And?"

"He thinks it might be fun to see what you come up with."

Walt received me as he sat in his walnut leather armchair, his layers of unwrinkled wool cardigans buttoned from top to bottom, each color peeking through the top of the other in a carefully-planned order. An old plaid Pendleton throw was draped across his lap. He wore fleece-lined corduroy slippers. His smoking pipe and the *New York Times* sat on the table beside him. Shelves of books looked down on us from every wall. A fire blazed in the fireplace.

"I drink martinis every day at 4 o'clock, and I have a girlfriend. Do you have a problem with either of these?"

I laughed out loud.

"Why 4 o'clock?"

"Earlier than that and I'd be an alcoholic. We eat dinner every night at 6."

"How long you been doing this?"

"The martini or the girl?"

I loved him immediately.

"It's been 4 o'clock martinis since the war. The girl since my wife died. Her husband died too. The four of us were friends for forty years. My wife told me to let her comfort me so I wouldn't crawl into the proverbial foxhole."

He chuckled. "I do what I'm told."

We began to talk freely, and it didn't take long for the past to creep into the present as he recounted his years as a soldier, most especially his attempts to make sense of it all.

During World War II, and again, when he was sent to Korea, he had written letters to his sister. In them, he shared his observations, feelings, and philosophical renderings about a world he called hell.

"It wasn't the war that broke my heart particularly," he told me. "I knew people would die. But the first time I saw a body thrown into the mud with all the other debris...Well, it broke me. I couldn't understand how a cause, even a good one, was worth throwing life aside like that.

"I went to World War II believing we could change the world if we fought hard enough. But then Korea...more bloodshed for the same underlying reasons. I lost faith that war could save anything. It felt so futile, so endless. I lost my innocence in all the mud."

The second Iraq war was in full stride as we talked.

"You see?" he said, pointing toward the newspaper. "The war that was to end all wars, and we're still fighting another one."

He'd become a Unitarian Universalist, hoping that philosophy, religion, and politics could intertwine to make the world a better place. Now he feared he'd failed. A life of social activism, and yet the wars kept coming. His fate was inexorably tied to that of the world.

"How'd you deal with the possibility that your life could be offered upon the altar of a cause? What did you fight for after you lost your innocence?"

He chuckled, "I'm going to die this time for sure."

"Yes, that's true."

"That's the real problem isn't it? All this fighting, and the world's the same. Only now I won't be around to do anything about it. How will I work for peace and justice then?"

He named his pain, what frightened him most about death, yet asked a question commensurate with the questions he'd asked and acted upon for sixty years.

When I returned the next week, he had a stack of Greek plays in his lap.

"I've got it," he told me. "Came in a dream last night."

"Tell me!" I replied with excitement.

"I'm going to catapult myself into one of the god realms. I've been looking them up to see which one might work best."

"And then what?"

"I'm going to join forces with them to make the world a better place. I just need a new body and a few more super powers."

"The gods can be a tough crowd," I chuckled. "They decapitate each other, throw spears of fire, ban one another to oceans or statues or, god forbid, mortal bodies. You sure you want to join that madness? There might be an easier path."

"I've made up my mind. Now help me decide who to saddle up with."

We spent the rest of our time looking at the archetypal characters of the Greek and Roman gods.

When he winked at me, a few plots into the conversation, I realized it wasn't about the gods at all. He was reorganizing his life one more time around the values of compassion and peacemaking.

A few days later, he began his final journey.

I arrived to find his girlfriend and two of his adult children supporting him as he shuffled slowly around the living room saying, "I've just got to get there...I've just got to get there."

I'd picked up the *New York Times* from the front porch on the way in and shook the rain off the plastic wrap somewhat ceremoniously. He looked up at the sound as we tucked a chair beneath him for support. I sat on the floor and read *The Week in Review.*

"It's a mess," I told him, as I read about the war, the campaign trail, the latest economic figures. "Thought you ought to know what's happening for your strategy session with the gods."

He smiled, a familiar twinkle in his eyes as he reached for my hand.

"I don't know how to find them," I said.

He nodded before the obvious dilemma.

"But I trust you can. Just keep putting one foot in front of the other. If you find solid ground, take a step. If not, put it somewhere else until you do. Just keep going until you get there."

He grinned ear to ear, even giggled, before saying, "I'd like to go to bed now."

He slipped into a coma shortly after we tucked him in and died the following day as his children sat at the foot of the bed swapping stories.

COURAGE

The linguistic origins of the word courage come from the old Norman French, coeur, *heart. "Courage is the heartfelt participation with life...(It) is what love looks like when tested by the simple everyday necessities of being alive."[12]*

Perhaps this is why Joseph Campbell chose to use the word hero, or heroine, to characterize our journey into what he calls bliss, or love—the soul's revelation of soul. We repeatedly stand upon the proverbial fork in the road and ask what we love most.

Tari once encouraged me to see the film, The Last Mohican, *and decide which character was most pure of heart. Naturally, I named the lead European-American character, fooled by his fight for good against evil.*

"No," she said. "It is the last Mohican. He is the only character free of distraction. His singularity of purpose eviscerated all else. That is the true nature of a pure heart."

Every wisdom tradition names compassion, bodhicitta, *as both the goal and the means for all our spiritual efforts. Whether we receive the kindness of teachers and saints or seek ways to give kindness, we invite all our expectations, needs, desires, even hopes and fears into a singular purpose. This tenacity of focus shears away or dissolves anything that might separate us from love.*

One time, I visited a house with conflict so severe that family members visibly carried weapons, eyed one another from different corners of the house, kept the children outdoors in case something erupted.

I had traveled there with a colleague to try and help settle things down, when a sibling confessed, "I just want what's best for him."

Another shouted, "Me too!"

We invited everyone to sit around the table, asking each person, "Is this true for you? Do you want what's best for him?"

Each person readily confessed their love, for it coursed beneath the fighting, alongside all the fear and anger. In naming this intention, their defenses began to drop, and we worked with the common purpose of giving the best to their dying loved one.

The dialogue shifted into an inquiry of what this might look like—the gifts each person had to offer, what their dying loved one might want or feel. We turned the focus toward him, and bit-by-bit they found practical ways to work with one another. They simply needed to be on the same side of the table with their eyes upon love.

This is courage. We focus upon the singularity of love, allowing it to pry our hearts open. We become willing to face whatever we must, even death.

❀　　❀　　❀

FOR MONTHS I ENJOYED the stories of a retired chaplain, "a man of the cloth," as he liked to say. As a young man, he'd been in the military less than a year when the freighter ship he worked on suddenly changed directions and sailed to Pearl Harbor. They were the first ones to arrive from the West Coast after the bombing.

During the war, he repeatedly held hands with the wounded and the dying, wishing he knew how to greet such suffering.

When he returned to the mainland, he trained as an army chaplain, serving in the Korean War soon after.

From the beginning we swapped stories, enjoying the camaraderie our parallel paths invited. As a brilliant storyteller with a persistent sparkle of laughter in his eyes, he spun evocative tales.

I always sensed that he understood my hunger to learn, and without judging, he told stories meant to teach as much as reorganize his experiences.

We whispered the iniquities to one another, those graphic things you only share with colleagues; pushed our questions through the limits of one religion or another; and shared a God more enigmatic than predictable.

One day he said, "We've never prayed together."

I laughed, saying, "Who wants to spoil a good story?"

He grinned.

We both understood that it was time to move into a new form of intimacy, free from the burden of words.

We never tried to find a common ground of belief or ritual, choosing to sit together holding hands, eyes closed, listening to the songs that naturally rise with such invitations. In these minutes that quickly became hours, we stopped wrangling our minds around the unspeakable. We were simply present.

From this point forward, he'd ask me how I was doing rather than what I was doing. I asked him the same. We stopped quoting scripture. He told me how it felt to hold the heart of another in his hands. I asked where he kept the grief. We'd return to prayer.

A few months later he was admitted to the hospital for breathing difficulties as anxiety seized his throat. His inability to speak aggravated his symptoms, until finally, they called an ambulance for help.

When I arrived I held his hands. Everyone naturally left

the room as the urgency dissolved into silence long enough for him to name the dilemma.

"I'm not afraid of death. I've seen so much. I'm ready.

"But all those men and women, I can see their faces, the blood, the panic, the weeping, the gasping, the choking..."

He paused looking into a world I couldn't see.

"Bombs fall...I run from one to the next..."

I waited as he rode the memories, expecting him to name his fear of death, when suddenly he shouted, "Oh no! I haven't prepared my wife for this! I've been so selfish! I haven't readied her for death! Only myself."

He wept, his body heaving from the effort.

"My dear friend, this is not a war. You will not fail her in death," I said, stroking his hand.

He caught his breath.

"I loved her for her courage, you know."

She'd waited for him through both wars when, first as a soldier and then as a chaplain, he'd walked through the thick of battle to care for others. She never knew what his work as a chaplain would demand of him, or whether or not he'd be alright, only that he had to go.

"She will call upon this courage again, and so will you."

He nodded.

"She is surrounded by loved ones," I reassured him.

He wept anew.

"I am no longer the one to care for her, am I?"

I didn't reply.

"Then this is the true death," he said. "I must allow others to love her now. It will no longer be me."

He wiped the tears from his face, took a deep breath, and sighed.

We slipped into a familiar silence.

It was mid-February, raining off and on. A low fog hovered over nearby hills, threatening to stay until sunset. His room was on the top floor, higher than any nearby buildings, giving him unbroken views of the winter sky.

His breaths deepened, the wheezing barely perceptible as he dropped into the hollow center, and asked, "Do you really think I'll be alright?"

I hesitated before what felt like a rhetorical question. Suddenly, the sun broke through the clouds, illuminating the grassy slopes in a surreal display of light and color. We gasped simultaneously.

"I lift up my eyes to the hills"—I recited, reaching for the small book of psalms I carried in my purse. *"From where will my help come from?*

"I look deep into my heart, to the core where wisdom arises.
Wisdom comes from the Unnamable and unifies heaven
and earth.
The Unnamable is always with you, shining from the depths
of your heart.
His peace will keep you untroubled even in the greatest pain.
When you find him present within you, you find truth at
every moment.
He will guard you from all wrongdoing; he will guide your
feet on his path.
He will temper your youth with patience; he will crown your
old age with fulfillment.
And dying, you will leave your body as effortlessly as a sigh." [13]

Still watching the dance of earth and light, I led him into a visualization woven from the psalm, the sky, his autobiography, and a God who'd been in every battle with him.

"He will not let your foot be moved; he who keeps you will not slumber..."[14]

As he climbed to the top of the hill, the sun faded behind the clouds once more, and he fell into a peaceful state of sleep and rest.

That afternoon his family took him home. Within an hour he entered the coma of dying.

The next morning, having made prior arrangements, I slipped into his living room without knocking. I nodded to his son, who sat on a nearby couch, hugged his wife, and sat beside this dear man, breathing with him once more.

Rain poured outside. Thick curtains darkened the room. A single lamp shone in a distant space like a candle. The house became a grotto. None of us spoke.

Then suddenly, he exclaimed, "It's more beautiful than we imagined," while reaching through the side rail of his hospital bed toward me without opening his eyes. I took his hand in mine.

"It's so beautiful," he repeated. "It's so beautiful."

"Thank you," I whispered.

Then he withdrew his hand and returned to his private prayers.

FORGIVENESS

A fellow chaplain once observed, "Forgiveness is at the heart of all we do. No matter how comfortable any of us might feel, there's always another rock to overturn."

"Doesn't forgiveness mean that at some point the path of Sisyphus ends?" I asked.

"Tell that to all the men and women still fighting with loved ones, buried beneath regret, or lost within denial and despair."

"Perhaps this is the process, not the end."

"I just wish people wouldn't wait until they die. It's so much harder in a crisis when pain, panic, and grief enter the mix."

Every professional I've ever met feels the same sorrow. The word forgive can feel more like a battering ram than a release. A home visit can become a gauntlet of entrenched miscommunication, desperate pleas, or even seething revenge rather than an opportunity for healing.

However, most of us have also seen the transformative nature of forgiveness, the magnitude of love. We've stepped into homes that feel like sanctuaries, as well as those that don't, sometimes in a single afternoon. It doesn't take very long to realize that death isn't the problem.

Yet, sometimes, I think real forgiveness isn't only for all the ways we've hurt one another, but also for the stark landscape of our humanity.

In any given moment, we can stand face to face with the tenuousness of life. Our bodies can crumble in an instant. Violence, disaster, or terror can eviscerate even the tiniest dreams. We cannot protect our children or loved ones from danger. We perpetually wrestle with our fragility, as well as all the clumsy and miraculous ways we treat one another.

Each of us is doing the best we can with what we know.

Perhaps this is the true nature of forgiveness—the capacity to include rather than separate, to see fellow human beings rather than good and evil.

Sister Chan Khong tells a harrowing story from the Vietnam War. Young counselors from the school she began with Thich Nhat Hanh were dragged to the river by soldiers, thrown to the ground, and then shot in the back. One survived long enough to recount the story.

When asked to give a talk at their funerals, Sister Chan meditated for three days while proponents from both sides of the war insisted she use her talk as a political platform. Unable to find words, she continued her prayers of compassion, until she remembered that one of the soldiers had said, "I'm sorry," before he pulled the trigger.

From these simple words, she chose to see a small window within the heart of an enemy, softening the boundaries between them. She thanked the attackers, recognized the vice of conditions within which they lived, and appealed to the tender places of peacemaking that could still utter condolences even within the horrors of war.[15]

Forgiveness engages a fierce vision of beauty that invites us into inequities. We release the temptation to fight or withdraw, and in so doing, slip into the clarity of possibility.

Love exists within us, just like everything else. In the blazing arms of forgiveness, we love—we are love.

❀ ❀ ❀

JACK LIVED ON several acres of land he walked and tended for most of his adult life. An avid gardener, he annoyed more than one professional as he stumbled down worn paths to water his vegetables each morning, despite the cancer now traversing most of his bodily systems.

"To tell you the truth," he told me one afternoon after I caught him watering all the roses his wife had loved before her death, "I wouldn't mind falling between one of those rows of vegetables down there. I could count the stars with my last breaths. Or close my eyes and listen for the coyotes. It's the waiting that's gonna kill me. I don't like tomatoes from the store. The roots need consistency or the fruit tastes bitter."

I wasn't the first one to think that he probably wouldn't be alive when the tomato plants bore fruit.

"The deer love tomatoes as much as tulips," he told me, pointing toward the lanky plants pushing through the top of each metal cage.

As he named all the varieties he'd planted that year, some from heirloom seeds he'd cultivated, I noticed he hadn't put up any fencing to protect his plants from the wildlife. I chuckled. He wasn't planning to be alive when the plants bore fruit; he just wanted to be sure that when the time came, the vegetables were "worth eating."

One day I arrived as his daughter headed toward the garden with a gathering box, a couple of hand tools, and a new nozzle for the hose.

I probably raised my eyebrows but didn't say a word as he whispered, "It's better for her this way."

He confessed an early life of alcoholism, years of recovery, and all that was required to make forgiveness a path of life, because "I'm sorry doesn't cut it when you've stolen your little girl's childhood...

"I don't want this to be hard on her."

His daughter had taken a leave of absence from her job and moved in with him as he steadily declined. "To give back all that he's given to me."

They played board games after dinner, shared favorite books, experimented with new recipes, read through old journals, and sorted through photos with a familiarity that belied the difficult years that once haunted them both. No signs of anger or shame remained.

Within days of releasing his garden into the care of others, he fell into bed as easily as tripping between the vines of squash, and barely spoke again—not from physical inability but more like a man in prayer.

"I just sit and watch him for hours sometimes," his daughter said on the phone. "I can't tell if he's dreaming, sleeping, thinking or praying. So I wait. Then, from out of nowhere, he'll say something pithy. Sometimes I don't understand him until a few more thoughts leak out, but I nod or give one-word replies. He smiles, takes my hand, and returns to rest."

On my next visit, the house emanated such peace that I instinctively took my shoes off at the door to his room and sat on the hardback chair beside his bed without offering any verbal greeting. For, like his daughter said, "It feels like church in there."

I joined him in silent prayer, contemplating the serenity that softened all the lines of his face, the steady whisper of his breath. I closed my eyes, when suddenly he whispered, "Hello."

His bedroom was spare, oriented more to the views out the

windows than any interior ornamentation. Though on this day, curtains blocked all light but for the glow of a tiny lamp beside his bed. Still, the room shone with an alchemical gold hue that seemed to radiate from the fluid pores of his countenance, as I could find no other source.

"You look like the burning bush of Moses," I replied.

He pointed at my shoeless feet, chuckling.

"May I continue to pray silently beside you while you rest?" I asked. "Perhaps, I can learn something of God through you."

He took my hand, nodded, and returned to his repose.

An hour or so later, when I told his daughter about our time together, she stopped me, saying, "Wait here, my husband has to hear this."

I recounted the story, describing the light and the way I kept thinking about the burning bush of Moses.

Her husband said, "A few days ago, as we sat together, he suddenly sat up in the bed and asked me to read him the book of Exodus. So I grabbed a nearby Bible, read the entire chapter, and before I closed the book, he asked me to read it again. He did this for three days. I've probably read him that chapter forty times."

"Christ said that where our treasure is, there our heart is also. Perhaps he is becoming the story of Moses."

A few days later, everything in his room looked blue, as though the ceiling had become the empty sky or a quiet mountain lake, revealing the watery depths beneath the rays of the sun.

He became a little more agitated, repeating, "Jesus, a fisher of men. Jesus. A fisherman."

"Yes, Jesus was a fisher of men," I'd reply.

After several minutes, the intensity of his declarations increased. He suddenly cried out, "My daughter!"

"Yes, she's in the living room. Shall I get her?"

"She needs to get into the boat!" he implored. "Before it's too late."

Then he grabbed my hand. "Please, you must talk to her before it gets too late."

"I promise."

He settled onto the bed once more and fell asleep.

This time, his daughter fought back tears as I recounted her father's words.

"He worries because I don't attend church anymore," she said, before sharing the events that led to her choice to spend Sunday mornings at home.

"I don't think it's church your dad worries about; he seems to be more upset with time."

She shook her head. "He can't possibly know."

When I asked her what she meant, she replied, "I have breast cancer."

She'd been diagnosed a few weeks before she came to care for him. She kept the news secret.

"Do you think he knows?" she asked.

"Are you afraid it will hurt him if he does?"

"I have been trying to be strong for him so he didn't have to be strong for me."

"But he's a father. I think he simply wants to know you'll be okay."

"I'd like to talk with him about God. He's so sure about it all—no doubts, no worries, just this persistent knowing. Watching him like this, he sees something we don't. You know?"

"I do."

When she told him about the cancer, he replied, "I know. I

always knew when you were hurt. I just haven't always known how to help."

A few days later, he fell into a coma. She sat beside him throughout the night, listening to each breath as he "melted into the pillow."

Just before he passed, he opened his eyes, took his daughter's hand, gazed into her face, and said, "It's so beautiful. I want you to know it's beautiful."

She believed him and never felt afraid throughout her chemotherapy treatments.

"It was as if he sat beside me, praying that I would see the beauty too."

FACING PAIN

I've noticed a welcome change in the mission statements of many hospice and palliative care organizations. In the beginning, eager to reassure families about the safety of dying at home, we promised that there would be no pain. We focused upon our capacity to comfort.

In doing so, each professional examined the question of pain and, like the familiar tale of blindfolded philosophers touching different parts of an elephant, offered our view of the problem and the solutions we could bring to the collective intention. Some of us offered to smite it, while some taught the strength to greet it. Some gave suggestions for ways to endure the inevitable necessity, while others engaged it, asking what story it could tell. We unknowingly reflected the various cultural and religious ways we manage pain.

With time, each of us learned to ask patients and families about their view of pain, not solely their measurements of pain. In doing so, we learned about their views of life and death, their motivations, beliefs, and needs. This was the elephant in the room—we treat people and families, not only pain.

As professional caregivers, as midwives, we choose to walk with one another, no matter what arises. This is what we're really promising.

So much weaves us together as human beings. How we feel in any given moment depends upon an array of senses, thoughts, emotions, and beliefs. This is true of pain as well.

If we focus solely upon pain, we inadvertently objectify it. We treat pain as if it were somehow separate from us. This can cause us to fight against it—and therefore, ourselves—or to feel helpless rather than capable. We feel alone, rather than part of a team of professionals who are well versed in what happens to our bodies and minds as we die. We silence anything that might be associated with pain, such as the lost, hurt parts that live within us too. We forget the context within which all experience, even death, occurs.

Yet, when we focus upon individuals and families, we enter the journey together and engage everything that arises, including pain. Together, we explore what works and what doesn't, potentizing all our medicines.

❄ ❄ ❄

DAVID LIVED IN AN assisted living home when we met. Cancer of the throat had required repeated surgeries and treatments that left him unable to speak or swallow food. We communicated by computer.

When cancer struck, he was studying to become a priest, a choice he made late in life following a lucrative career.

"Maybe I should have chosen to be a priest when I was younger," he typed.

"Hard to say what effect prayer might have had earlier. Seminary isn't only about one's vocation," I replied.

We began a lively discussion of the interrelationship between one's private heart and one's offering to the world when I asked, "Did you want to be a priest to find something you didn't have or to give something you could no longer keep to yourself?"

The bantering stopped. In the silence, I feared I'd gone too far. Then he typed, "Maybe that's the nature of a wounded healer. I entered seminary battered and broken, banking on a few scriptural promises, giving everything away for a sense of peace. I would have served the best I could."

He'd divorced when his wife fell in love with one of his oldest friends. His children chose their mother in the ensuing battle.

"I thought I could start over, go back and become the man I'd wanted to be before I fell in love and started a family.

"Now look at me. This room is smaller than the dormitory I lived in, and my roommate thinks I'm a religious nut. My children live a couple miles from here, and we still haven't seen each other.

"Seminary brought me right back to where I started with less than I had before."

"Perhaps your prayers were answered after all," I suggested.

"How's that?"

"One way or another, healing still calls you. You've been stripped to the bare necessities."

"And still looking for a way to stop the pain," he concluded.

One day the nurse confided that both he and his pain were becoming unmanageable. He'd report that his pain levels were fine in the morning, and then call after dark, panicked by pain he could no longer manage. The problem was magnified by his inability to speak, for he had to be mentally alert to type and, therefore, ask for help. At least once, he'd been rushed to the emergency room when he ignored his pain so long that he fell to the floor unconscious, lying there until his roommate returned from dinner to find him.

These perpetual crises would be unnecessary if he would only dialogue about his pain and medications. This was the issue. Staff wasn't sure if he was lying, playing games, or had an undiagnosed cognitive impairment that was impeding his ability to make good judgments.

That afternoon, I dropped by on a hunch that something else drove his behavior, for despite his overt religious practices, the constant conversations, even preaching, he'd never really shared much about his personal, spiritual experiences.

I began with a sincere concern for his safety.

"You know," he typed. "The nurse has been through this already."

I nodded. "I'm just looking for common ground."

"You want to know about my pain don't you?" he asked.

"Yes. It seems so black and white, like you don't use medications and then suddenly you're on your knees, nearly blacked out and in desperate need of help. There's a logic here I'm missing."

He smiled like a Cheshire cat, and for a second it felt like a game.

"Your entire life, every moment of your day is lived for God. So tell me, where does pain and medication fit into your philosophical view?"

He paused, assessed me once more, and then pulled out a small, wrinkled pamphlet from the drawer beside his bed and asked me to read it. The booklet gave a prayer cycle, with instructions to read a sequence of petitions. It came with a promise that if someone did this daily for a period of three years, one could experience union with Jesus.

"There comes a point," he typed, "in which you realize heaven is never very far away. The real goal is to see the world like Christ, to identify so completely with him that we disappear. Heaven is merely the beginning. This," he said, pointing to the pamphlet, "is the real goal."

For more than two years, he had imagined himself crucified upon the cross. He did this first as an offering to God, and then as a gift to all who suffer—to anyone in pain and in need of

God's comfort. He followed graphic, even gruesome descriptions as a template for this visualization, teaching himself to engage the experience of Christ directly.

He'd never missed a single day, even after surgery. In fact, he had included each medical treatment as an opportunity to identify with the sacrifice and suffering of Christ.

"Is this what you pray when you're in pain?" I asked.

"No, I pray this, three times a day, like the instructions teach, and I remember Christ when I hurt. But when the pain begins, I pray for the souls in purgatory."

He showed me another prayer card he used then. As his pain increased, he chose to identify with the love of Christ for all beings rather than his own pain.

I understood. It wasn't actually pain or even the passion of Christ he had been contemplating, but a love that could be offered despite the consequences or circumstance. A compassion that existed with the pain, not apart from it.

Rather than take medication to stop his discomfort, he chose to dedicate his pain to the wellbeing of all, most especially those he feared were trapped between the worlds of earth and heaven.

I shared my understanding, and he typed, "Yes, you get it." Then, with tears in his eyes, he clutched my hands.

After a few minutes of silence, I replied, "The only problem I have is the harm this causes to staff and your roommate. If you fall or pass out or die in a pool of blood, they live with the consequences. They need kindness as much as the souls in purgatory."

This time he saw our dilemma too.

"You know our pain scales, right?"

He nodded.

"So tell me, on a scale of 1 to 10, at what point are you no longer able to pray for the souls in purgatory? At what point does the pain prevent you from reading, remembering, or reciting the words clearly and with sincere intent?"

He held up seven fingers.

"Then perhaps we can make a deal. When the pain reaches seven, you'll ask for pain medications and take them. Until then you pray undisturbed."

He agreed.

Things went a little more smoothly after that, for all of us could work within the nobility of his quest, and he now included staff and fellow residents in his aspirations of kindness.

I cannot say how these prayers connected to the release of his own sorrows, especially the regret around his family, but as he approached the last hours of his life, his eldest son arrived. After more than a decade without any communication, he now sat beside his father who was resting deeply within the coma of dying.

The week before, David knew he had very little time and recognized that he might die without ever saying goodbye to his children. He'd added them to his prayers of pain, when his petitionary prayers had produced no results, wishing that his suffering would be compensation for all their mistakes.

"I want them to be happy," he told me. "I want them to know forgiveness. I want them to know God loves them, that I love them. I will pay what price I can on their behalf."

I shared these words of love with his son, as he stroked his father's hand.

"I'll take communion when the priest comes," he said. "In honor of my dad, I will forgive too."

The sages of many wisdom traditions say that we can hear

all the way into death. I believe it, for within seconds, David opened his eyes and turned back the force of death just long enough to join his son at the ritual table. It took about twenty minutes to wiggle back into his upper body, stretch his fingers, and type clearly.

As soon as he was able, he hugged his son, both of them weeping, while I scrambled to find an available priest at that late hour. When I returned, their wet faces exuded a radiance of love no less wondrous than sunlight poking through thinning clouds after a week of rain.

Following confession, communion and guided prayers, David re-entered the path of dying.

His son was praying at his side when he died a few hours later.

MERCY

One day I joked with Tari about how I was going to quit psychotherapy and open a flower shop.

"Why a flower shop? Why not a café?"

We began to fantasize, trying on the outfits of every job that would garner tangible results, generate a lot more pleasure, and offer significantly higher pay. I simply wanted to close the door to my office, pretending that if I don't see it, it doesn't exist. I wished for a more normal lifestyle.

As we became more and more irreverent, she casually interjected, "Death is a great mercy."

The joking stopped. I wasn't sure I heard her correctly.

"Death is a great mercy," she repeated.

People raced through my head. The nurse, whose thirty-year-old husband dropped to the floor from his chair, taking his last breath before she could lift his head for CPR as their three school-aged children watched. The parents of a carload of high school students who had died instantly in an accident, only months before graduation. The young woman brutally murdered by her husband.

She didn't speak. Neither did I. Tears trickled down my cheek.

Then Tari added, "Without death, we would feel unsafe. Life would be unbearable. Death comes when we need it most. One day you'll understand."

Growing up, the word mercy always seemed to be affiliated with receiving something I didn't deserve, what none of us deserved. It felt like the shadowy sidekick of grace, meaning it helped but didn't feel good. This face of Divinity did what was needed to be done, whether we cooperated or not. It was the necessary power of transformation.

I've wondered about a life free of death. Unlike Hollywood, I can't find an oasis apart from a changing desert. Without death, we would be bound to our own creation, frozen upon the limitations of our conditions. The world would stop moving, and I wonder if we could even breathe without the release required for any inhalation.

When death enters, it cuts the interdependent cords holding our lives together. This includes all the constituents of our bodies and minds. The entire operating system collapses.

Perhaps this is what feels so uncomfortable—death isn't something that happens to us. Death occurs within us. Regardless of the cause of death, we can't defend ourselves, or fight it off, or run and hide because we are dying. What we've identified as me or I, dies.

Yet perhaps this is also the mercy—death strips us bare and begs us to look into the eyes of change and ask what remains. We search the bowels of impermanence for the nature of existence itself.

※　※　※

ONE TIME I TRAVELED to a state mental hospital with a fellow hospice nurse to visit a man diagnosed with paranoid schizophrenia that was so severe he required 24-hour, one-on-one care to ensure he didn't hurt himself or others.

He could not differentiate between a hallucination and a nurse trying to offer medication, for he experienced all phenomena like an array of unidentifiable flying objects that he assumed were harmful simply because he couldn't track its source, and therefore couldn't stop it. He could only defend himself from harm and, as such, lived in a constant, hypervigilant state, responding violently to any unfamiliar stimulation. He'd slap friends and strangers alike, spit and kick at the first sign of danger. The nurse felt it would be better if she accompanied me to our first meeting.

As soon as we entered the room, we found him thrashing in the bed, rising and falling, twisting and flailing, and even from the doorway, we could see the purple of his toes, fingers, and lips. He was in the throes of dying.

She immediately headed toward the nurse's station to get the proper medications, saying, "Go do your magic."

I tucked my bag into a corner, pulled back my hair, and explained to the staff member what was occurring. Unaccustomed to death, he hadn't recognized the symptoms, assuming his charge was merely agitated.

I began by standing in the center of the room, just within visible range of his peripheral vision. I entered the rhythm of his movements, his breath, his journey, like a young girl joining a jump-rope game on the playground.

"I'm going to pray with him and see if I can help him settle while the hospice nurse gets the medications, okay?" I said to the staff member.

He nodded.

I slowly moved toward his bed, scraping my feet across the linoleum and humming softly so he could hear my approach. He continued to sit up and lie down, twist and turn, swat away invisible flies, when suddenly, he became still and smiled.

He looked at the ceiling, the dusty walls, the half-opened blinds, his fingers, his palms, the sheets, the blanket—like someone awakening from a long bout of amnesia.

The processes of dying had cut through the physiological wires of his disease, dissolving all the schizophrenic symptoms that once ensnared his mind.

"Do you know what's happening?" I asked, now standing beside him.

He nodded, turning toward me so we could communicate directly.

The staff member gasped.

I matched the rhythm of my breath to his. "Just pray with me," I offered. "We'll do this together."

I placed my left hand upon his heart and began to recite the Lord's Prayer, for I'd been told that he was a devout Catholic man.

He took a deep breath, and sighed, the way a child does after a storm of crying.

We held eye contact as I whispered each phrase synchronistically with the rhythms of his slowing breath.

When the hospice nurse returned with medications, his exhalations were more like yawns, opening into long stretches of stillness. She moved to the other side of the bed, shrugged her shoulders and whispered, "What?"

A trusted colleague, I asked her to support me.

She nodded and joined the rhythms of shared breath as he continued to release more deeply.

Just as he was about to close his eyes, a doctor, accompanied by a medical team pushing a crash cart, rushed into the room, threw on the overhead fluorescent lights, and started shouting orders.

Instinctively, the nurse and I grabbed one another's hands across the bed and over his chest, as if to protect him.

My friend yelled, "Turn out the lights. We don't need that," pointing toward the crash cart.

As the doctor joined us at the bedside, I continued my recitations with each exhalation, inviting him into the rhythms too, saying, "Please, let him have this. Give him this dignity. He's better in this moment than he's been his entire adult life. I have him. I promise."

He nodded and everyone became silent. The lights went off. No one stirred.

"Our Father
"Who Art in Heaven
"Hallowed
"Be
"Thy name…"

We sighed collectively.

I held vigil as the staff came to say goodbye. A priest offered his blessings. Residents came as well.

When everyone left, detectives interrogated my colleague and I in order to document the cause of death. As we waited for them to come, we quipped in classic black humor, "Should we say death by prayer?"

No medications had been given. Technically, we hadn't done anything. We didn't have to.

I AM STILL HERE

An anthropology professor once asked our class, "What is a human being?"

We spent a week on the topic as he argued, rightfully, that how we see someone determines our treatment. He pointed out the racist, misogynist, and demeaning language used to justify such horror as slavery, genocide, rape, and abuse. He noted how our personal stories, even of intimate family, could hold more weight than current conditions. We treat people according to our encoded perspectives.

He felt that we could change a great deal of our cultural issues if we could simply sit with one another and explore an expanded definition of a human being that includes all we once considered as other or different from me or us.

"In common spaces, we learn how to see the world through eyes other than our own. We learn as much about ourselves as we do the ones we're listening to, for in order to listen, we must first change. They become more of who they are because they no longer need to fight against our preconceived notions. Together we become a little less afraid and a little bit more open."

One pressing view in our culture is the ingrained assumption that we exist within our capacity to imagine existence or think. "I think, therefore I am."[16]

Words are associated not only with communication but also intelligence, our capacity to think. We rely upon words to develop concepts and to tell our stories, equating who we are with our capacity to do so. We equate existence with the operating system, and all the ways we believe this system should function.

I feel this is why we are so quick to say, "That's not my mom anymore," or "My husband died years ago," when familiar words or conversations cease, as conditions like dementia unravel social contexts. We don't think someone exists without language or words.

When I began visiting those no longer able to speak, I learned how much of my training relied upon words as well—whether to process emotion, to ask questions, or to study truth. We counted upon conversations to heal and even to pray.

Yet something new occurred when I spent time gazing into the eyes of each person with a curiosity born from the compassion of namaste. *I would commingle breath, breathing in and out according to their rhythms, listening deeply to their personal songs.*

It felt uncomfortable at first, to enter into a conversation without words, but with a little practice, I became aware of all the subtle expressions inherent in each breath, glance, or bodily movement. I learned to release my own feelings, expectations, even the need to diagnose, fix, know, or seek. I looked past the words, stories, and assumptions to see who might be gazing through their eyes. I taught others to do the same.

Within this milieu, things happened that defied all assumptions about both disease and words, for we leaned into what I can only call soulness—the unique ways life moves through each of us regardless of outer appearances. We entered the shared space of existence.

❋ ❋ ❋

When I first met Dan, the facility aid took me down a flight of stairs and wound me around two corridors to the last room of an unlit hallway.

As we walked, she prepared me for what we'd find.

"He stares at the ceiling all day. Never looks at anyone. Doesn't move or blink."

He had no roommates and hadn't left the confines of his bed for nearly a decade.

"We just go in there to feed him or change his sheets, but otherwise, we let him be. It wouldn't matter anyway; he doesn't notice anything we do."

His room was stark like a monk's cell. White walls. Windows and curtains closed. No television, radio, art, photographs. No special blankets or other personal items.

I was a little afraid I might startle him, unsure of how all the months of quiet had affected him, so I became still too. He was clearly well cared for and, knowing the women in the facility, loved as well.

I opened the curtains to look out onto a private garden of spring flowers, and then sat in a large leather chair and waited. His breath was the only sound in the room—sturdy, studied, regular. Strong like a steady bellows.

His religious background was Christian, a sect that frequently turns to the Bible. So perhaps I held this filter, for soon, I could hear the Beatitudes singing within each breath. I wondered if Christ had ever seen Alzheimer's like this.

I recited the lines aloud, the words intermingling with his breaths as if we were singing a duet.

Suddenly, he jerked in the bed several times, surprising me. He shook his head back and forth upon the pillow, then kicked both legs violently without bending his knees.

"I see your legs kicking, your head shaking," I said, now standing next to his bed.

We made brief eye contact; then, just as suddenly, it stopped.

We returned to prayerful silence.

On the way out, I told the facility staff what had happened. None of them had seen him move in more than two years.

In coma therapy—work meant for those no longer able to verbally communicate—movement like this isn't judged as good or bad. Rather, it is considered a response driven from untethered subconscious material that is now expressed along the neurological pathways still capable of response.

A reaction like this indicated that something about the scripture reading penetrated his consciousness, as did the simple acknowledgement or witnessing of his physical response. This would be a place to explore further.[17]

The next day I visited his wife.

"He loved the teachings of Christ," she smiled. "Taught many classes on the Beatitudes."

Turned out he'd been a theology professor whose specialty was hermeneutics, the study and interpretation of the Bible.

I asked her permission to read to him, and subsequently did, sometimes several afternoons a week, whether I saw a movement in him or not. Most of the time I didn't.

I enjoyed our visits, as a natural rhythm unfolded. It was our own private liturgy. I'd breathe with him for a little while, then open the curtains and windows as songbirds danced through pruned trees, squirrels buried their treasures, bumble bees and all the other flying insects chimed in.

We'd share the cacophony of quietude together. When feelings or imagery rose within me, I'd read the matching Biblical passages.

One afternoon, only a few words into a Psalm, he turned, thumping his head against the pillow so he could see me. Then I saw what could only be described as a clearing of fog, as though someone had blown the veil off his countenance, revealing the sun behind the clouds.

He could see me. Hear me. Understand every word.

Experience told me it wouldn't last long.

As fast as I could, I rattled off how much God, his wife, and family loved him, that he was not, and never would be, alone, and then I recited the verse that came into my mind, "Be still and know that I am God."

He smiled.

I stopped talking.

He continued to smile, intentionally gazing into my eyes. Five seconds. Thirty seconds. Two minutes. Three. I simply smiled back.

Then, just as quickly, he returned to the inanimate expression that had become his norm.

A few days later he entered the dying process. With the support of the nurse, his wife came to say goodbye.

This time he woke not only from the haze of Alzheimer's but also from the coma-state of dying long enough for her to say, "I love you," and for him to mouth the same words in return, kissing each other one last time.

POETRY

Native Middle Eastern mysticism, scripture—or language of truth— can be understood literally, metaphorically, and universally.[18]

Each sacred phrase, word, or prayer begins in our conceptual mind, working its way through our feelings and beliefs to penetrate the resonance of our souls. They sing the songs of Oneness, the beauty of awareness and our place within it all, piercing any shell of belief that may separate us from knowing this.

Yet Neil Douglas-Klotz explains that many of our scriptural translations, especially of the New Testament, are based upon Greek renderings, which separate the body, mind, and spirit—a philosophy not held by traditional Middle Eastern culture, and most likely not by the quoted sages, Christ included.[19] *This can hold true as we translate sacred texts from other cultures and religions also, especially when languages like English lack words for unitive expressions common in other worldviews.*

From such a separatist view, the soul becomes an object either separate from the flesh, pining for a new home, or it doesn't exist at all. We reduce truth to an ideology, theory, or litany of beliefs— stories we hope will carry us through the valley like a torch in dark places. We focus our efforts upon these beliefs, forcing ourselves or others to fit within their prescriptions.

Unfortunately, this doesn't help when our minds slip past the capacity to form words or even understand them. We cannot think ourselves into death.

Perhaps this is why it can be so difficult to know we are dying.

Why we need doctors to tell us the journey of our own souls. Why we argue when they tell us the truth of our condition.

We have separated from our own ephemerality, tucked ourselves into calculated boxes, surprised when someone threatens the safety of our container.

Maybe this is why our scriptures are filled with poems and songs.

"Poetry's work is the clarification and magnification of being. Each time we enter its word-woven and musical invocation, we give ourselves over to a different mode of knowing...to the increase of existence it brings."[20]

These words are like midwives, bridging the known with the unknown, expanding our world view, our minds, and our hearts to include it all, even death. We live within the garden, walk across the valley, climb the tallest mountain—free from the bondage of knowing too much or too little. Chocolate lilies, ancient oaks, bubbling brooks, endless seas, the old barn down the road, the gleaming curve of the highway, the pile of stones on the corner...all invite us into the arms of awareness, knowing this was the teaching all along.

ANNE LED AN exemplary life. A respected elder in her church, she taught bible studies to children, prayed with women at the local jail, and led a women's group for new members. Each day, she spent hours pouring over the Bible, dissecting words from their Latin, Greek, and Hebrew roots, memorizing lines she wove into a tapestry of hope and truth she could offer to anyone in need. When I'd visit, she'd teach me the latest verse from her studies and invite me into a conversation meant to uplift us both.

One day the nurse called, asking me to visit because Anne's

anxiety wouldn't relinquish, even with medication. She was declining rapidly, and had awakened that morning with the sudden inability to walk across the room unaided, her body heavy, "like wet concrete," fatigue bearing down. Her mind felt slippery, and she couldn't concentrate. Thoughts and sentence fragments rolled in and out of a mind no longer tucked neatly into its own paradigms. She felt disoriented and panicked by the inability to reorient. Fear slipped through a lifetime of answers she could no longer recall.

She thrashed on the couch where she tried to sleep, unwilling to return to her bed. As she hollered and shouted, I quietly sat on the floor beside her. Sometimes she'd pause, as if listening or catching a thought, then tangle and untangle her feet beneath a stack of blankets, pause, and struggle to get comfortable once more.

After about ten minutes, she suddenly noticed me. Pointing toward her Bible, she cried, "I can't read it anymore. I can't remember the words."

I volunteered to read for her, but she yelled, "You don't understand!"

"I'd like to understand and will try my hardest, but I'll stay with you even if I don't," I replied.

She glared. I remained as still as possible when she cried, "What if it isn't true?"

"If what isn't true?"

"The Bible."

I had no reply.

"I did everything right," she cried.

"Yes."

"Everything according to the Bible." She paused. "But what if I missed something? What if none of it is true?"

"Have you ever felt God?" I asked.

"What?"

"Have you ever felt the presence of God?"

"I don't know what you mean."

"When you close your eyes at night where do you find rest?"

"I don't. I just keep reciting Bible verses until I fall asleep."

"Then it's time to pray. It's time to live the Bible verses. You no longer need to remember them."

"I don't know how to pray anymore."

"It's alright. I do."

She wrestled with an inconsolable anxiety for the rest of the weekend before slipping into a deep coma. As the new week began, we were expecting her to die at any time. Then the nurse called, saying she'd awoken in a somewhat shocking fashion.

Despite every medical sign of imminent death—unconscious, no movement, limbs blue from lack of blood flow, breaths more than a minute apart—she suddenly opened her eyes as if she'd seen or heard something, as if she'd come across a blocked road and simply reversed her direction.

Bit by bit, she reanimated her body from the top down. She'd wiggle one fingertip, then another; a toe, then another; as though she'd never felt a body before. By the time I arrived, she could move her lips and both hands.

As soon as she saw me, she mouthed, "Bible."

I grabbed hers and read from the gospels, the psalms, the pages with her scribbled notes and markings, but nothing comforted her. She'd cry, stare, mumble, and sleep with open, vigilant eyes; her body stiff like a plank; her pallor grey, lifeless, yet somehow alive. She remained in this state for nearly a week.

One morning, I found her gazing at the ceiling, whispering as if hosting a private conversation, when I caught the phrase, "No, I need words."

Whatever death looked like for her, it lacked the promises of words. She could not find God anywhere else.

So I sang one of the laments of David, about the harrowing grief of a soul who searches without finding. I sang words of fear, doubt, sorrow, and longing. For a little while she listened, momentarily closing her eyes as I slowly invited her into her heart by naming the pain aloud. Her calm only lasted a little while. I kept visiting twice a day regardless, repeatedly inviting her into her own experience.

One morning, I sat beside her in silent prayer as the unceasing dialogue, even arguments, began again, and this time when she said, "Bible," I replied, "You will know when it is finished. You already know what you need to know. Listen for when it is finished."

She stopped talking and looked at me with a quizzical expression, as if she never thought it would end, as though she believed eternity would be like this.

For over an hour, I'd say, "It is finished." Pause...then, "Listen, you will know."

She'd wait, talk to the ceiling, then listen again as I guided her into her own journey.

I will never know if she remembered that Christ's last spoken words were, "It is finished," or if something about the singing, the invocation, unspoken compassion, or time shifted the war, but she finally closed her eyes. The tension drained from her body as she sank into the bed once more. This time she passed without any visible arguments, as though it really were finished.

DREAMS

A friend once remarked, "The soul's language is poetry. In our deep places, we speak in metaphor, if we speak at all."

As we die, we naturally become poetic as we seek a means to communicate what cannot be said. We sink into the feeling stream of our process, now manifesting more like dreams. We describe what's happening more often than our thoughts about it. Language becomes a metaphorical bridge.

"It's burning in here," someone might cry in response to a fever. "It's flooding," another might pronounce in response to a leaking catheter bag, while another might shout, "It's breaking. It's breaking," as she describes the sensation of dying.

This can feel disconcerting to witness, for it can seem like hearing the dialogue of a movie without any images. We don't really know what our loved ones are trying to say, or whether or not they are alright, for we don't share the same context. We're not sure how to respond.

In graduate school, a psychology professor taught that to help someone no longer capable of communicating directly about thoughts or feelings or needs, we must join their "dream." In other words, we listen to all the disconnected strands of communication and piece them together as though they were an accurate reflection of their experience. We learn how to drop didactic thinking just long enough to see the world through their eyes.

He taught that it wouldn't help to argue about whether or not the dream was true because it was true in a client's eyes, in the same way that we believe all the stories of who we are or who our family is. The only difference is that these clients can no longer pop out of their dream to discuss the narrative for they are caught inside them, unable to revisit what the rest of us might call consensual reality. For them, change cannot occur in a discussion about the dream. It must occur within the dream itself.

To demonstrate this, he shared the journal entries of a schizophrenic man. It was a series of wild tales of log canoes, rainbow-colored drivers, houses burning on the shore, a narrow strait through which the lead boat could escape, and an elderly woman asking for coins at the gate. As we listened, he encouraged us to treat the loosely woven images like one of our own dreams. Who are the characters? What are the symbols? What is the message, the pain, the question, the need? How might we greet these if we were a character in his movie?

This training proved invaluable in my work with the dying, for there comes a time when death dissolves the boundaries around our familiar sense of self. Our ability to dialogue, or even engage between subject and object, blurs into a single field of play in which we are within our own dream. Everyone is in our dream. We cannot separate.

To communicate, we enter the dream, give according to this logic, and trust the natural unfolding.

✺　✺　✺

AFTER A DISABLING BOUT with pneumonia, an elderly woman was moved to a new bed in her facility. Soon after her transfer, she became extremely agitated. She grabbed at and clutched every staff member or visitor who entered her room, screaming when they tried to leave. Nothing anyone said helped her frantic fear of being alone in her room. Yet she screamed each time someone tried to help her. Nothing seemed to work, and when her hollering disturbed other residents, they simply closed the door, exacerbating the problem.

When I entered the room, I paused at the door to watch as she pulled her covers off as though to get up, then pulled them back up to her neck as though tucking herself back into bed. She'd pant from the effort and begin again. She repeated the actions with such exactitude and rhythm, it almost appeared to be a practiced ritual.

I pulled up a chair next to the bed but didn't speak as the facility staff had observed that conversation intensified her discomfort.

All of a sudden, she turned toward me and cried out, *"Ma mère…Ma mère."*

She grasped my forearms, imploring once again, *"Ma mère!"*

"Ma mère?" she repeated. (Where is my mother?) *"Ma mère? Ma mère?"*

"Ma mère est ici," I told her. *"Votre mère est ici."* (Your mother is here.)

As I stood to repeat the words, she grabbed me and pulled me into a hug across the rails of her bed before I could stop her. She tucked herself into my arms. I cradled her, singing the only French lullaby I knew. As she cried like a frightened child, I rocked her, adding the simple consolation, *"Votre mère est ici. Votre mère est ici."*

She softened, and I caressed her head against my shoulder the way I would any weeping loved one and added the prayers of Mother Tara in Sanskrit.

"Om Tare, Tuttare Ture Svaha. Om Tare, Tuttare Ture Svaha."

I continued to hold her as she released her pain.

After ten minutes or so, she pulled her head back far enough to see me. *"Ma mère est ici?"* she whispered.

I nodded.

"Ma mère est ici," she repeated. *"Ma mère est ici."* (My mother is here.)

Then she lay back onto the bed. I re-tucked her bed covers, and she fell asleep. All signs of agitation ceased.

The next day, even the temporal symptoms of cognitive impairment disappeared. She asked a staff member, "Where did you find a French-speaking priest?"

When the staff member couldn't answer (as no priest had visited), she said, "Say thank you for me. I liked the singing."

She died peacefully a few days later.

PRAYER

I've come to think of the wordless places as prayer, as if all the holy songs lead here. Perhaps it's the way silence reveals the need to unburden our minds and hearts of the accumulated clutter, showing us how to do so. Perhaps it's the invitation to rest. Perhaps it's the welcoming embrace of timeless love.

Neil Douglas-Klotz teaches that the Aramaic word for pray is shela. *Aramaic is the language most modern scholars believe was the common cultural language Christ spoke.*

The word shela *can be translated in two ways.*

First, it can mean to incline or bend toward, listen to, or lay a snare for. With devotion, we lay a snare for inspiration or wisdom to arise. We evoke a feeling of depth or spaciousness. We create space for the sacred.

The second possible translation is the image of a canopy or veil in which the sacred provides shade or shelter from the immense, uncompromising, perhaps even the terrible, burning face of reality.[21]

Prayer is often associated with death as a means for entering the pregnant spaciousness of spiritual experience, invoking the healing balm inherent in doing so. We find solace within the refuge of an open heart. We taste the communion of shared space.

As Brad DeFord taught, "The goal of every session is prayer."[22]

We follow each invocation into the ever-present presence.

Yet, sometimes, prayer is used as a Hail Mary pass for a desired outcome, or as a means to fly a white flag, or a way to force someone into fevered beliefs. Perhaps this is why so many of us avoid prayer. It feels like the revocation of control, a diatribe of belief rather than a path of possibility.

Chagdud Tulku Rinpoche said, "Praying is not about asking; it's about listening...It is just opening your eyes to see what was there all along."[23]

We may begin with our fear, our disappointment, our heartfelt wishes, our unbridled need, or our unanswered questions, but with time, even these can melt into the pool of kindness abiding within the spaces of any heart. This is the true purpose of prayer: to evoke all the natural qualities of beauty hovering within the contours of any storm and know them as our own.

❋   ❋   ❋

A NURSE INVITED ME to join her weekly visit with Lillian, an elderly woman from Georgia, who'd driven away just about everyone with a life review that inevitably ended with scathing blame and dismissal.

I arrived in my best vintage suit, the highest spiked heels in my closet, and a matching purse on my elbow, looking for the one connection that still held interest for her.

When the nurse pointed out my shoes in an attempt to encourage a conversation between us, Lillian asked me, "Do you vacuum in them?"

I laughed, "No. Did you?"

She showed me a photo, tucked into one of the bookshelves, taken of her seventy years earlier in a bathing suit and three-inch black patent pumps.

"You were a knockout!"

She smiled.

For weeks Lillian told me about every dinner party, afternoon tea, social gathering, and party she attended—starting with her earliest childhood memories. She recounted how she forgot to put the dessert spoons on the table, or could never get the white linen napkins clean enough, or forgot to invite one of the neighbors to her coming-out party. She criticized every menu, recounted every fallen cake, every social misstep.

Then she would launch into the care at her facility, the size of her apartment, how the stove wouldn't turn off, the way everyone looked at her in the dining hall. She pulled at small wrinkles in her skirt, fiddled with hair that wouldn't hold its shape after a nap, tucked her feet beneath a blanket to hide "ungainly ankles," swollen from the toll of spreading cancer. It was like listening to the super ego gone mad—all of us felt small.

Yet, beneath the weekly rants, a small, childlike self, buried within an elderly frame, simply wanted to know why her son didn't visit anymore. She wanted to know whether or not she'd failed.

She approached the Bible and God with the same disparagement. She wasn't too happy with a world that let people die before their time. God had failed too, but she was afraid of Him. She wanted to see her deceased husband, not the rings of fire.

One day, as I contemplated our visit, I heard a niggling voice within me that didn't want to listen to her complaints anymore. Determined not to withdraw from her as others had done, I sought a middle ground.

I told her, "I am not big enough to help you. I cannot repair your past any more than you can. Perhaps we should ask God to help us."

She paused, raised her eyebrows, chuckled, and asked, "What did you have in mind?"

"Let's make a list of questions for God. Let's ask God to help all the people you fear you've wronged, as well as all those who have wronged you."

From that point forward, we spent our time together preparing for prayer, slipping from the outer world of right and wrong to an inner one full of emotion, longing, questions, and need. We'd spend an hour or more creating her list.

Then we'd pray for her son as she imagined what he might need, rather than all the ways they'd failed each other. We prayed for her grandchildren, what she hoped they had learned in their lives, and the legacy she wished to leave them. We prayed for the facility she slept in and the nursing aides she feared would abandon her. We asked God to become involved in her personal life rather than cavort with the criticism that beat her daily.

One day I arrived and she said, "No lists today. Just prayer." We held hands as she wept. "I'm dying. I'm really dying."

Then she showed me a New Testament verse from the book of Corinthians that said, *Love never fails.*

"Do you think that's true?" she asked.

"Let's take this to prayer too," I replied.

A week later, she slipped into the coma of dying. Her hair still coiffed, bed sheets tidy, she lifted her ear from the pillow as if listening to her grandchildren gossip between bites of burgers and fries, even reaching for the paper bag. She still seemed to notice each time someone new walked down the hall past her room.

I breathed with her for a little while, before whispering in her ear, "Lillian, it's time to go to prayer. It's time to pray."

First, she lifted her eyebrows, and then she smiled as I repeated the reminder for prayer. Her breath softened immediately. As she settled more deeply into rest, I whispered, "Love never fails. Love never fails."

She reached her hand toward me one last time. I kissed it. She turned toward the valley within.

I sat with her for another hour. She never stirred again, dying quietly a few hours later.

HEALING

Time can lose linearity around the deathbed as the past collides with senses softened by biological change, upending how we store coded beliefs. Memory, emotion, cyclical thoughts, or unbridled fear, can slip through the crumbling walls to reveal everything our psyches tuck just out of reach.

It's similar to a house built brick by brick, stone by stone to create a life. Each window is the lens through which we view our days, colored by everything we hang upon the walls to adorn our building. We live within this confined view without much thought until an earthquake shakes the structures hard enough to reveal the foundations of our lives.

Death is such an earthquake—as is long-term meditation and prayer—for they dismantle fragile structures to reveal a view much larger than a single house or operating system.

As everything collapses, we can fixate upon all the rubble, or we can gaze through the tines of history into the open sky and release. One leads to suffering. The other to freedom.

To enter this space even once, we touch the suchness of existence. This changes our experience of everything else. From this view, the spiritual path is quite simple—we taste the nature of being and release anything that obstructs our capacity to do so.[24] We remember our own nature. We know ourselves through the eyes of awareness, as awareness.

In death, we are managing both the whirlwind of the earthquake and the inherent invitation to leap into the spaces, regardless of whether or not we have meditated or prayed. It can feel both overwhelming and confusing.

For most of us, this means that healing comes when we attend to the whirlwind of the earthquake while acknowledging the spaces." We comfort the unbidden confrontation with the sudden revelations of our unconscious, the vulnerabilities of bodies, the veracity of death. Simultaneously, we do what we can to lead one another into the spaces, for here the debris simply floats unhinged, or dissolves like salt in water, or returns to the soil like particles of dust—it simply releases.

❋ ❋ ❋

JACK TURNED THE horrors of war into a life of service to his family and community. A gentleman, he said yes to my visit, but then politely refused to entertain any questions, choosing to read the newspaper instead. I threw a little small talk out now and then between the long pauses of empty conversation, which I regarded as normal, rather than a refusal.

Then, out of the blue, he asked if I played the piano.

"In grade school, a little in college."

"Play me a tune."

"It'll be one-handed."

He shrugged his shoulders. So I played an old show tune. He clapped in rhythm and stomped his feet, surprising me with his sudden participation, telling me to pull the music books from the bench and play from them.

I scrambled to sight-read each page, doing my best to keep a steady rhythm of melody. Before long, he started singing so loud his daughter ran in from the backyard to see if he was alright.

She laughed, "Oh, he loves to sing," and sat down to join us. With Christmas approaching, more and more family appeared each week to sing with the "piano chaplain." Grandchildren turned pages and offered their own concerts.

He never answered a single question because I never asked one. We simply sang, laughed, hollered and shouted each tune as if on stage at a neighborhood theatre.

One afternoon, his daughter walked me to the car, saying she hadn't seen such emotion in years.

"He's a war veteran," she explained. "Saw worse things than he'll ever speak. He survived the Death Marches in the Philippines for two years as a prisoner of war." She shook her head. "You'd never know it. I can't remember a time he ever raised his voice. But we could always tell when he was remembering. He'd sit in the same old chair he's in now and get real pensive, disinterested in anything—even a ballgame on television— and when it passed, he'd join us for supper. We all love him so much. But he never lets us in. How did he keep all of that under control for so long?"

A few months later, as he entered the final days of his life, we found out.

The nurse and family were trying to help Jack into bed, but he fought so hard they feared he'd broken his daughter's ribs.

When the nurse called me to come help, I implored, "Put him back in his wheelchair."

"He's too weak, we'd have to restrain him so he wouldn't fall."

"He survived the Death Marches," I told her. "He thinks you're trying to kill him. The dying process has returned him to the war."

A social worker had explained to me that to survive the Death Marches one had to remain standing. If someone fell down, they were tortured or killed. For two years, Jack survived by staying upright, witnessing the untold horror of those who could not.

When I arrived, he was slumped over in his wheelchair, held in place by sheets wrapped around his torso. He stared at the floor without moving or speaking.

I settled onto the floor in front of him, so he could see me without lifting his head, and hummed one of his favorite hymns. Every once in awhile, I added a familiar phrase of encouragement to the chorus until his eyes softened and he could engage me directly.

"Do you know what's happening?" I asked him.

He nodded, never breaking eye contact. I could feel the dissonance of war in each breath, but also our connection.

"Jack, I need you to show me how strong you are. I need to know your strength so I can count on you."

I stood up. "Push me as hard as you can."

He tilted his head back to see me and stared.

"I'm serious, Jack. I need you to push me. I need you to prove your strength to me. I need to see it. C'mon. You can. I know it. Show me your strength."

A fierce determination rose, the one he had harnessed all those years ago.

He snapped his shoulders back and threw himself into attention, like a soldier saluting the American flag. I stepped toward him as he pushed against my torso with all his might, almost knocking me over. He pushed for nearly three minutes until he had exhausted all his physical ability. It was a remarkable feat of courage, for between the medication and the dying process, he shouldn't have been able to move, much less fight anything.

Then he began to weep, collapsing against the sheets, as I sank back to the floor, gazed into his face and hummed. I never touched him, offered no comments or reassurance. I trusted the silence, the music, for I suspected that this was the place he rested his mind for those two long years as a young man.

"I'm going to cut a deal for you."

He smiled, as though he knew something about me too.

"I'll ask the nurse and your family to find a way to keep you in your wheelchair, but I need you to fight to stay here."

He suddenly became serious, and I worried he wouldn't follow my reasoning.

"Jack, you already survived the war. You don't have to go back anymore; it's over. But I need you to focus your mind here with all your strength. With every ounce of courage, I need you to stay here. You must fight to stay here."

He released a few more tears and sighed.

"The war is over. You can be here with your family now."

He smiled, took my hand and squeezed it, almost as if to "shake on it."

He passed the following day with no further medication, sitting in his wheelchair. The healthcare assistant they'd hired had rolled him into the kitchen as she made lunch. She turned to stir the soup, and when she looked back, he'd died while his grandchildren and great-grandchildren were playing nearby.

We all stood together in a circle holding hands, a child on either side of the wheelchair as we sang Christmas carols on a sunny April morning and prayed, each of us saying thank you.

OUR BODIES KNOW

As I explored the work of birth midwifery, I trained as a doula, so I could emotionally support women in labor. As part of my training, I attended births, sometimes with local midwives.

On one occasion, I came to assist the midwife, as well as the mother, when extended family were unable to arrive in time. As labor intensified, we all hovered close to support the mother, who suddenly struggled with pain.

The birthing mother, Susan, kept trying to crawl out of bed as if labor came from the sword of an invisible perpetrator she couldn't get away from. We'd encouraged her, held her hand, offered a multitude of interventions meant to help her both concentrate and rest, but she became more agitated. We all sat back and gave her space.

When this didn't work either, the midwife moved closer, touched the top of Susan's foot, and just before the next contraction said, "Find my hand."

As the contraction swelled, she took an exaggerated breath, held it, caught Susan's attention, and exhaled just as loudly. Susan focused for a minute, squirmed, then stared at her midwife as she wrestled between her desire to run and her desire to feel her midwife's hand, her own foot.

"Here," her midwife said. "Here," encouraging Susan to focus upon the sensation in her foot, until she finally let out a breath it seemed she'd held for twenty minutes.

The stale air suddenly shifted.

"Now here," the midwife said, touching Susan's ankle as the next contraction began. She nodded, focused upon her ankle, and breathed like a determined marathon racer until the contraction released, then fell back onto her pillow panting.

"When the contraction begins, breathe in," said her midwife. "Yes, that's right. Feel my hand. Here, that's right. Good. Now release."

The midwife now held both ankles, and this time, Susan began to breathe through the contractions as well as between them, riding a single stream of contraction and no contraction with each breath cycle.

Then the midwife placed her hands gently on Susan's belly. "Here."

On the next contraction, Susan sank into her own body with a thud and rode the wave like a dancer. No one else stirred as she inhaled and exhaled, rested, sang, paused, intoned, like a bamboo flute calling out in the night. We silently breathed with her, followed each turn as she receded into some deep interior place from which she birthed her baby with a howling crescendo and a burst of laughter.

Over the years, I've seen many people try to climb out of their beds as if death were a thief grabbing their ankle. It is an understandable response to want to run from the inevitability, to grasp at anything available to avoid the consummation.

Yet if we can sink into our bodies, the unitive vessel of our experience, it can lead us bit by bit into the truth of our predicament—we cannot escape.

To embrace this, to embrace the fullness, our bodies become midwives.

We are both mother and child.

❈ ❈ ❈

ONE TIME, A NURSE asked me to visit a man with long-term dementia. We'd met several times before, usually in the commons room of the facility where he enjoyed watching old movies with other residents. He had a buoyant disposition, smiling frequently, willing to participate in most any activity.

That morning, he'd slipped into the coma of dying.

He was tucked into his bed with a quilt sewn by his family. Soft music played on his tape player. He was calm, quiet, peaceful. Staff didn't need to do much more than check in on him.

Then, in the afternoon, a group of schoolchildren visited the facility. They brought handmade gifts and walked through the hallways singing Christmas carols. When they arrived at his room, they sang a common song, not worrying whether he was awake or asleep.

Yet, when they sang a chorus referencing heaven, he sat up and began to howl, startling everyone. When staff couldn't calm him, they called hospice.

The hospice nurse offered him medication, which quickly settled much of his agitation, but he still moaned periodically as if in pain. When she learned about the connection between his discomfort and the word heaven, she wondered if he still had unanswered questions and asked me to visit.

When I arrived, he was lying quite still in the bed, yet oddly lucid, like someone who wakes up from a dream unsure of where they are. He followed sound, movement, and light with vigilant eyes but offered no other obvious response.

I breathed with him for awhile, until he noticed me. We held eye contact until his hands unclutched the sheets. Then he smiled.

I touched his heart with my ring finger and waited as his mind located the sensation.

"Here," I whispered.

He nodded.

We breathed in sync for several minutes as he located my finger.

Then he sniffed the air and cocked his head as if trying to hear something.

A few more breaths and he filled his heart space like water filling a well.

Still holding eye contact I whispered, "Yes... here... yes."

We breathed together for several more minutes as the spaces between them lengthened.

We were still gazing into one another's eyes as he released.

HONESTY

When I became a hospice chaplain, I often tried to sugarcoat death, feeling this was the way to alleviate anxiety. Yet our wisdom traditions often take a different approach.

"You see, death is a very real experience. Usually, we do not connect with a sense of reality. If we have an accident—or whatever happens in our lives—we do not regard it as a real experience, even though it may hurt us. It is real to us as far as pain and physical damages are concerned, but still it's not real for us because we immediately look at it in terms of how it could be otherwise." [25]

A fellow chaplain once asked, "Why do we always say, 'It was a peaceful death?' Every single time, no matter the conditions, we say it was peaceful, even when it was difficult. When we all knew it was difficult. I think we're missing something in our need for consolation."

"Perhaps we don't understand the word peaceful. Perhaps we do not yet understand what we fear," I replied

"Then honesty demands we ask."

David Whyte teaches that "honesty is not the revealing of some foundational truth that gives us power over life or another or even the self, but a robust incarnation into the unknown unfolding vulnerability of existence, where we acknowledge how powerless we feel, how little we actually know, how afraid we are of not knowing, and how astonished we are by the generous measure of loss that is conferred upon even the most average life."[26]

When we cover death up, even with our best-intentioned stories, we bury the pools of courage dwelling in our depths that seek answers within the shattering truth of our lives.

Rachel Naomi Remen, in her book Kitchen Table Wisdom, *begins her collection of healing stories by acknowledging the inherent potency streaming through any one of us. "After listening to hundreds and hundreds of their stories over the last twenty years, I think I would have to say that most people do not recognize the strength of the life force in them or the many ways that it shows itself to them."*[27]

Perhaps the key is hundreds and hundreds, for when we repeatedly sit within the chrysalis, eventually what remains is the beauty of every life. The wounds and scars become part of this story, not the story itself.

Honesty is the means to unwrap this treasure.

✹   ✹   ✹

MELONY WAS A SMALL WOMAN with a brittle bone disease that caused pain with every movement. The structures of her body bent and broke like dry kindling beneath her own weight. It hurt to smile, to swallow, to breathe.

A devout Christian Scientist, she struggled between the demands of her body and religious interpretations that were at odds with her discomfort. She believed the use of pain medications would excommunicate her from the church.

Faced with an impossible choice, she took the medications and grieved with every pill, hoping such an act was forgivable, that *she* was forgivable for what she saw as cowardice, insufficient convictions, and sinful behavior.

As we explored her pain and the need for forgiveness, she

insisted that only a practitioner from her church could pray. To be cut off from church was to be cut off from practitioners. To be cut off from practitioners was to be cut off from prayer. To be cut off from prayer was to be separate from God.

She felt constant fear and shame. She blamed herself and expected everyone else, including God, to do the same.

We explored a multitude of means for reconciliation, but in the end, she closed the subject. I asked her to teach me about her tradition instead.

Each week, she read to me from a book written by her church founder, Mary Baker Eddy. She prepared for each meeting, reexamining familiar passages so she could share their meanings with me. She felt safe doing this since it was a publically available book. Anyone could read it.

One day, she pulled a worn piece of paper from the back of the book and read it aloud. She'd memorized the passage more than forty years before. She recited it every night before she went to bed and every morning when she awoke. She now found herself meditating upon it throughout the day as other thoughts and worries dissolved into her contemplation.

"Will you read it again? It's beautiful."

She did, emphasizing each word the way a priest might read a holy invocation.

"These words just take you all the way in, don't they?" I replied.

"Indeed."

"It feels like prayer."

We held eye contact as tears began to stream down her cheeks.

"I've never been strong enough," she confessed.

"I've always been too stubborn.

"I've tried so hard for so long.

"I still feel so much pain."

We waited in silence.

"A minister once asked me why I didn't call upon grace more often," I said. "I'd grown up thinking everything was my responsibility, even things that weren't."

She nodded.

"I thought about the question for a long time and realized I'd been trying to be good enough for love. I never liked how naked I felt, how the vastness exposed my smallness. I wanted to be so much more."

She took my hand.

"I do not think God depends upon the unpredictable nature of human beings. We are the ones who find refuge in the storm," I concluded.

From that time forward, I'd arrive for a visit to find a chair placed directly in front of hers. She'd take my hands. We'd close our eyes, and she would recite the passage. Then we would quietly sit together, sometimes for an entire hour.

One day she asked if I would read these words to her "when the time came."

I wrote the passage down and then left copies in my car and wallet, placed it into medical charts, and gave it to all the on-call nurses, for we agreed that when the time came and she could no longer recite the words alone, one of us would offer them to her as a reminder of all she already knew.

"We are not elders in your church, but we are spiritual friends."

Several months later, she entered the coma of dying. That afternoon, I silently slipped into her room.

Without a single identifying sound, I sat beside her once

more. Within minutes, she smiled and said, "I knew you'd come. I just knew it."

I read her the passage of scripture one last time.

SURRENDER

David Whyte describes a crisis as the clash between interior and exterior in which all the qualities of an ever-growing human being greets all that threatens to overpower it, whether through forces we deem outside of us, or the forces of our own interior. We examine all the thoughts, feelings, and stories we carry even as our conditions demand we release them. We ask how we can shape our world with what we know. We are shaped by our world. We walk the edge of this exchange throughout our lives, until in death we recognize a single flow.[28]

Perhaps the soul is like a river running through the middle, navigating the material of inner and outer on its journey to the ocean.

Zach tells me that the existence of rivers relies upon an interdependence of soil, weather, and plants. The rocky soil determines how much water can pass through without sinking into the mud. The climate determines the amount of water. Plants create the skeletal structure that holds banks together before the rush.

Before we erected dams, sometimes our great rivers would spread out for miles into floodplains that would feed soil for future growth. Sometimes they would restructure with each decade or century of change, creating new tributaries or carving new passageways to travel. Sometimes they would intensify their surge to the ocean, taking the topography with it.

Regardless, the river persistently zigs and zags across the countryside in a delicate balance with all that it feeds and all that feeds it on its long journey to open waters. Perhaps this is the life of a river. Perhaps death occurs when water dissolves into water at the oceanic edge. Water has been water all along.

I doubt a river ever considers the need to surrender to its own journey or even wonders who or what it is when it pours into the ocean, but as human beings, we ask many questions.

People often say, "I will not or cannot surrender to death," or "I don't like the word surrender." I believe they are standing on one bank or the other, eyes fixed on willow trees, tumbling rocks, and weather reports, hoping to dam the waters. We intuitively understand that to leap into the river will carry us away from familiar ground.

This is what we're surrendering to, the movement itself. The movement of water into water. We are like babies inching down the birth canal. Death is simply the force pushing us through.

❊   ❊   ❊

ONCE, A MAN TOLD ME that the only tolerable thing following his wife's death was that he didn't have to attend church anymore. We were sitting around an old formica table in his kitchen as the wind blew through a Magnolia tree out the window. It felt a little awkward for both of us until we began talking about flowers. We walked to a small deck off the back of the house to see his pots of peonies and the expansive view of the valley.

"Have you read all those books?" I asked on our way back to the kitchen, pointing to a hallway of filled bookshelves.

He smiled and walked me through a library of Western writers and more books about rivers than I'd ever seen in one place.

When I came the following week, I brought my favorite collection of poems by Jim Harrison and a few by Richard Hugo, western writers who also loved rivers.

He welcomed the literature though remained mostly silent. I wasn't sure he liked hearing the poems, until he asked, "Have you ever listened to the way a river moves without moving?"

I shook my head no.

"People are always moving on their way to somewhere. But rivers always move, and yet they are here. I had to get really still to see this one."

We laughed.

"It's like that," he said. "You can learn everything you need to know sitting by a river."

Each time I visited after that, he'd share more wisdom like this, drawn from a lifetime of traveling across the U.S., then Canada, South America, and even Egypt. For nearly four decades, he walked rivers, sloughs, and springs; he sat on the banks, listening to what he called "The Great Mysteries."

"They're like people really, with a recognizable quality that makes you feel at home, on familiar territory, and then suddenly, they surprise you, taking a bend through the terrain that makes you wonder what happened, what history of events pushed them through the mud at just that angle."

On a wet winter morning, a few days after he walked me along the Danube, he slipped into the coma of dying.

I brought his favorite collection of Jim Harrison poems and sat beside him, listening to the rain, the wind, the draining storm pipes, and the ripples of fluid in his breath.

I closed my eyes when all the sounds of water became synchronistic, one following the other, and thought, "He sounds like a river."

I could imagine the thick white waters in the center, surging past boulders; the quiet eddies near the banks with the bubbles of fish feeding just below the surface; the trickle of spring waters atop mountains; sloughs rising and falling with each tidal turn.

Suddenly, his live-in caregiver burst into the room, breathing heavily, frantically trying to find what she thought was a leak.

"Do you hear water running?" she cried. "I've looked everywhere. It sounds like it's coming from in here."

As she ran into the bathroom to check all the plumbing, which she'd done in every room in the house, I closed my eyes once more, listening carefully to all the songs of water to be sure of what I was hearing.

When she returned she stood next to the bed, hands on her hips, bewildered, and asked, "Where do you think it's coming from?"

I felt a little nervous, but motioned in such a way as to acknowledge the sacred nature of the deathbed, glancing toward her friend several times until she understood.

"Oooooh," she said, as I pulled out a chair for her. They'd shared stories about rivers as well. Nodding toward me, I knew she could hear it too.

I began to sing softly, weaving a line from the first Psalm and another from the book of John, with a little bit of Jim Harrison—celebrating, recognizing, joining him in the living waters.

"Praise be to Jesus," his friend said. "Praise be to Jesus."

He was no longer a man who loved rivers. He became the rivers he loved.

ONE MOUNTAIN

The forests where I live are filled with dense evergreens, nourished by nine months of rain and the extreme sunlight of dry northern summers. Tree trunks are broad—limbs layered with needles, moss, lichen, and fallen debris. Seedlings sprout on fallen trees as easily as on the ground.

In the long stretches of winter, two or three steps into the trees can eradicate even the smallest fractions of daylight, for the sun skirts too closely to the earth to break through the walls of green. More than once I've followed deer trails through the dripping corridors when I couldn't locate the barely-traveled human paths, as all sense of bearing dissipated within the perpetual blur of fog and flora.

The first time this happened, when I was unable to find my way out, I looked down at my feet, saying, "One can only walk in circles for so long."

I created a make-believe labyrinth, circling wider and wider from a beginning forged from the only spot I knew—the place where I stood.

With each turn, I studied patterns of bark, owl droppings, and sullen puddles. Listened to ravens, the whir of wings, tracked their winding trails through the trees. I noticed rock piles, the contours of each hill, a hidden ravine, the curl of tree roots. I familiarized myself with the forest, circling and circling, until I reached a familiar path.

Eventually, I climbed beyond a single ecosystem of trees to my house atop the hill, where windows allowed me to see the entire landscape. In every direction, the same sky blanketed my little world, the neighbor's, the island, the ocean, and the entire globe. We all hovered together upon the very same mandalic crust beneath a single sky.

A Buddhist monk, pointing toward a large mountain peak, once told me, "There are many ways up the mountain, but there is only one mountain."

Perhaps we simply need to find our footing and remember where we stand.

※ ※ ※

I MET WITH A COUPLE who came on hospice sequentially as their health quickly declined. We met weekly for several months until their personal home health nurse started refusing my visits, saying they had "no time." Commenting about this to staff, I found they were refusing social workers too. The nurse and home health aid were allowed, but only between episodes of the television show *Bonanza*. Their new daily schedule revolved around the six or seven times a day the reruns aired. They even rescheduled their meals, showers, and naps so they wouldn't miss an episode.

I thought this was an odd turn of affairs for the former university intellectuals and asked a friend what he knew about *Bonanza*.

"Good fights evil and wins, every time. The good characters are good. The bad ones always get caught. The ones in between learn how to become good. By the end of each episode, the world finds balance."

I asked a few more people for their opinions. Greeted with

enthusiastic, even passionate responses, I felt *Bonanza* might be like any other popular mythological tale. I just needed to learn the theology. So with the help of staff, we put all the characters into a coherent story of good and evil. I returned to their home after I agreed not to interrupt during an episode.

We silently watched television for an hour or so as I compared my new philosophy with the day's reruns. When the commercials came between episodes, along with a snack, I casually made a comment about Ben Cartwright. Both of them simultaneously turned from the television, the husband saying, "Why yes, I think so too."

His eyes twinkled as he recounted all the episodes that proved the theory.

"Do you watch *Bonanza* too?" he asked.

"No, just a few reruns when I was a kid. But I'd love to watch it with you."

"I'd like the conversation," he replied.

After several weeks of lively dialogue, they shared how the characters reminded them of Christianity.

They'd never shared their faith with anyone, preferring to attend church on holidays, and otherwise remained silent, for Christianity was woven into personal histories they also held privately.

He, his wife, and infant had narrowly escaped Communist Europe, just before orders for his arrest and execution were given. He'd refused to sign the necessary papers of concession to the new government.

Landing on foreign soil, he worked in a shoe factory while each of them retrained, piling graduate degrees one atop another to carve out a new life. Their resumes became history lessons, for the diaspora of cultures repeatedly became forks in the road that they wove into new paths. Their stories were the stories of war, participation, and redemption.

As he approached his last days, his mind drifted through time and place—landscapes mixed with people until east and west became a single story.

At the end of his bed hung an oil painting that he had smuggled out of the country in his daughter's crib basket, along with a few blankets and other family heirlooms. He'd received it the week they left as a gift from the artist, a childhood friend. A few months after their escape, his friend was tried and publicly executed for refusing to sign the same papers.

"So many died," he whispered. "So many died."

The painting portrayed a street intersection, less than a mile from his family home. Behind it the land rolled green and grey. The city street looked garish. The fork in the road was exaggerated in such a way that it didn't matter which direction one looked—it always returned to the lush landscape.

"Maybe he knew he was going to die," he mused. "I should have been there to help him."

The stories tumbled out—about his neighbors, family members, fellow scientists, librarians, bookstore owners, the town baker, friends lost in death when they refused to lie.

"They would have killed me too."

He stared at the painting.

"Now there is no one left to walk with me across the border. I ran away from home, and the faithful returned to the soil."

"Guide me to the crossroads," I suggested. "Lead me to the hills."

Together, we walked through the village streets of his homeland. We passed the neighborhood storefront. The backyard where his family shared Sunday picnics. The blacktop of bouncing balls and schoolyard disagreements. The church spire. Forgotten graves.

The aroma of baked bread wafted across the street, melted chocolate too; the smell of oil paints from a studio, damp wool, dusty roads. Snippets of conversation broke through. His mother's laugh, the priest's certainty, the whispered needs. Folk songs, wedding dances, Easter hats, oral exams, gunfire, bombs, armored tanks, foreboding silence, a crossroads.

He paused.

"I never really left."

More silence.

He glanced at me, the painting, me.

"Yes, we still walk together.

"Yes... yes... yes..."

I visited one more time but this time we sat together in silence. There were no more words.

He died a few days later.

HOME

As I write, our world is filled with people who have lost their homes or are seeking one. Hurricanes, fire, war, poverty, and politics have shifted the landscape so completely that refugees and immigrants on every continent seek the simplicities of clean water, safe housing, reliable medical care, the means to care for their families, and the ability to live in community with friends who share the values that bring meaning to their lives.

Regardless of our cultural backgrounds, home tends to be the hearth of our lives—a place of refuge, intimacy, and kindness that defines us as often as we define it. We struggle to leave these cultivated places even when necessity demands it, and when we must, we usually rebuild them as quickly as we can.

Yet home has always been more than brick and mortar. We live in relationship, not only to people or a defined space, but also to the land itself.

In my travels, I've noticed how people reflect their climates— skin the color of seascapes, bodies the shape of sultry nights, wrinkles circling eyes accustomed to squinting in the sun. Home is part of us, not merely a place to live. Our cultures, families, thoughts, feelings, dreams, and longings reflect this.

Around the deathbed, we frequently talk about home. Our inquiry about existence leads us to wander the halls of belonging, the seeds that blossomed into our lives, the ground to which we return.

In these places, I understand the cliché, "Home is where the heart is," for it becomes difficult to separate the person from the landscape. We are elemental beings.

As we die, we release the pilgrimage of our lives and return to where we began. We gather everything together just long enough to give it away and melt into the paradox of being, like a resolved koan.

❅   ❅   ❅

WHEN I FIRST MET ED, his 95th birthday was just a few weeks away. He challenged me to a game of dominoes and won all five rounds.

"Didn't think I still had it in me, did you?"

We'd play each visit, swapping stories that quickly grew into tall tales.

"Well, I once climbed a tree nearly 50 feet tall, no 100, no 200...without ropes."

"I swam across the lake, the big one, the great one...in December...without a wetsuit."

We'd laugh as he beat me handedly, even though I tried. We embraced the thrill of friendly competition, and before long, he began to slip a few anecdotes about his life into the mix.

After serving in World War II, he re-entered the country through San Francisco, where all army personnel were quarantined on Angel Island for six months. He slept, ate, and talked with fellow soldiers as they processed the horror and loss of all they'd faced. For six months, they received medical and dental care, as well as the luxury of rest.

Ed found many new friends, and honed skills better suited to civilian life as he watched the comings and goings of the sea. Near the end of his time, a colleague invited him to work at a nearby facility outside a naval base. As a young man drafted out of high school, he'd never imagined a reliable income, housing, and benefits, so he accepted.

He soon met a "lovely" woman. They married, raised a family, and never left the area. His great-great-grandchildren still visited him each week.

One day, I arrived for our visit to find him in bed after he caught pneumonia. For the first time in his life, he no longer had the strength to get up. He tossed and turned in the bed like a "trapped wolf."

"No games today," he announced when I sat beside him. "No more games."

We held hands as he stared toward the ceiling and shared the rest of his story.

He'd grown up in Oklahoma on the land of his forefathers, which was purchased before the civil war and before future laws that would have disallowed his family to buy, own, or possess private property. Against all odds, they'd maintained the entire acreage through war, famine, and persecution. He, his father, and grandfather were all born in the two-room house, which is still maintained by relatives.

"My father and grandfather died in the same house I was born, and now I am going to die here, the land of strangers. I am so ashamed."

He wound back through the decisions he made as a young man. The allure of a job with benefits, the pride his parents felt when he bought his first house, how he cared for his children, and when he sent his daughter to college.

He accepted the ocean but grieved his life apart from the dry plains and rolling hills. He had unknowingly lived in diaspora, both home and not home, during all the years since the war.

"Tell me about your land."

"In the north sits a single mound, a large hill, not quite the size of a mountain. As a young boy, I'd run to the top without stopping, lie on my back, and watch the clouds. A creek runs around the eastern slope. The wildflowers turn the valley purple each spring. I would even catch a fish or two when they languished among a few reeds catching sun rays. They'd get lazy like the rest of us in August."

He chuckled.

"Winter pierced the bone. Summer warmed the blood. Everything was quiet, calm, alive.

"We were quiet, calm, alive.

"Cougars watched. Snakes too. Sparse trees became friends we took care of, you know?"

He began to drift into the dream of memory.

"Memories live there. The soil knows.

"The water releases.

"And the sun...the sun...

"It is warm. Yes, it is warm...It is... "

He fell asleep, still holding my hand. I stayed with him a little longer, contemplating his stories and where he now lived. The window opened onto a parking lot. The white walls were unadorned. The only sounds were the cough of an old electric heater and traffic. We were so far from anything natural.

I called his daughter, who happened to be visiting his original family home at the time. She took dozens of photographs of the land, the house, the creek, the oldest trees, and blew them up to poster size. When she returned, she hung them on every wall, even the ceiling, so he would feel surrounded by home.

With each subsequent visit, he'd take me on a journey through the landscape of his childhood.

War, family, prejudice, church, rifles, shovels, ants, enemies, wolves, sheep, friends—all ran across the same hill once climbed by that forgotten little boy. He sat beneath the same gnarled tree, sipped from the same pond, circled a temperamental sea, walked this same room where we now sat.

In his final days, he'd gaze at the ceiling that now had a photo of the family home in California, alongside an old worn Oklahoma hill, and hold his right hand over his chest as if he were about to say the Pledge of Allegiance.

I don't know what his family did with the photographs when he died. Perhaps they're hanging on the walls of another family home, telling stories to the next generation. Perhaps they were burned, the ashes buried in the soil with Ed's.

LOVE

A minister once taught that in the book of Genesis, the Hebrew rendering of Eve's childbirth doesn't point toward the physicality of birth. Rather, it identifies the sorrow of all parents who realize that their children enter a chaotic, complicated, frightening world, on an unpredictable journey that will one day end in death. The great pain of birth is our inability to change this.

Some cultures offer funereal ritual at birth to remind parents of this truth. They name the pain as a means for recognizing the preciousness of life, encouraging parents to include this wisdom in their care.

Yet I'm not sure we can ever fully prepare someone for the death of a child or any other loved one. They are so much a part of our lives that to see their death is to see our own.

Perhaps this is what the ritual points toward, for love demands an unbearable confrontation with truth. To support the growth of another we give them into their own lives. We cannot keep them within our grasp. We destroy something precious each time we try.

I've often felt that death requires the highest qualities of love, for we learn how to give even as we release our loved one. Despite sorrow, exhaustion, and uncertainty, we leave our needs, our desires, even our hopes and fears outside the door, just long enough to love someone onto a path that will no longer include us.

I think this might be why survivors tend to ask about the after-life more often than the dying, as if we want to imagine our loved one's new life, discern if they'll be okay, and wonder whether or not they will still exist. We want to know about these tender strands of love that held us together for so long. We want to know what happens to us in the midst of change.

In the novel, A Tale for the Time Being, *one of the main characters, a young teenage girl, describes the funeral rites of her beloved great-grandmother, a Zen nun. After they clean and dress the body, they lay "a little knife on her chest to help her cut her remaining ties to the world."* [29] *Then they offer gifts she might need for the afterlife and nail the coffin shut.*

Nao wonders if her grandmother accomplished all she had wished for, whether or not she still thought of her, and where she went, for she can see that who she called her grandmother was no longer present. You can hear her say, "Now what?" with each new question.

A few days later, forgiveness entered the room as quietly as her grandmother once did. She and her father talked about the harrowing stories of their lives—not only the brutality once buried within the necessities of living but also the subtle philosophies of truth and hope, the private meditations that kept them going. Wound together across the time of generations, they found a strand of redemption that existed in the bones of their own secrets.

As they revealed these confidentialities, I couldn't help thinking that the beloved nun had expanded into the purity of love now coursing through the broken places of her family.

Perhaps it is in the ephemerality that love bears fruit. It peeks through the cracks of broken hearts to warm us all.

❈　　❈　　❈

I RESPONDED TO a call after a 24-year-old man was admitted into a nearby nursing home. He was in his last hours, dying from alcohol poisoning. Fifty or sixty friends and family crowded into the room, crying, raging, arguing, and grieving.

His mother was easy to find. Surrounded by several women, she was the only one in the room who kept a watchful eye on her son. I introduced myself, asking if I could pray silently. She nodded without offering conversation, and so I quietly settled into a chair about ten feet from the end of his bed.

He was in a coma, but I could follow the rise and fall of his breath easily, for both the inhalation and exhalation were sharp, heavy with effort, as though he pushed and pulled against compressing weights, the sounds almost artificial with each surge of effort.

I listened to what felt like a tugboat upon choppy waters, catching the ongoing rhythm before leaping into the spaces— those moments of rest between all the effort.

For three or four minutes, I offered a clarified silence to the pauses. Suddenly, I felt a tug, like someone grabbing a rope to climb out of a pit.

Simultaneously, the young man opened his eyes, turned to look at me, even lifting his head from the pillow so he could see me. We gazed into one another's eyes as I bowed slightly in acknowledgment before he collapsed onto the pillow once more.

His mother darted to his bedside, swept hair from his cheek, kissed his forehead, then pulled up a chair beside me.

"What did you do?"

"I simply prayed. Would you like to join me?"

She nodded.

I taught her how to breathe with her son so she could tell him one last time how much she loved him in a language he could still understand.

The entire room became silent.

The weeping, the gossip, the accusations, the angry questions, stopped for more than an hour as, one by one, more people joined us, focusing their attention upon him.

All around the room, people stood, leaned against the wall, and sat on the floor, inhaling and exhaling, reciting familiar prayers.

I never offered a formal invocation or ritual prayer, nor taught the crowd how to behave with respect and kindness around a deathbed. Only two people in the room knew who I was or why I visited. Everyone followed, nonetheless.

They stayed with him like this until he died, enfolded in a nest of love.

COMPASSION

One afternoon, a fellow chaplain came to my office incensed by a patient who fell three times in one morning, insisting God had healed him. His wife wept as she cleaned up yet another wound on legs swollen to twice their size. His children argued about what to do. Everyone yelled, "You're dying!"

Brian simply yelled back, "I am not!" got up, and fell again. Then they yelled at hospice.

Since God was mentioned, the chaplain had been called in as another voice of reason.

"Can't he see he's dying?" she implored.

I listened as she shared the details of her meeting with the family, as well as her frustration, for Brian rejected every philosophical possibility of what healing might look like in the face of death.

"He can't walk. He can barely breathe. He's covered in bruises and open wounds that will never heal. His muscles are like stones he can't lift. Every scan shows more and more tumors. He's fighting fatigue like it's an enemy. We keep telling him the truth. Pointing out all the evidence, but he can't hear it."

"Why do you suppose everyone's yelling the truth, even you?" I replied. "More and more yelling, and still it doesn't work."

We both laughed at the absurdity.

"Besides, why must you be the one to tell him he is dying? Why should anyone?" I asked.

I could see her frustration rise again, when she pleaded, "Why can't he see it?" Stating the obvious truth that his suffering existed not in death, but in the fighting.

"Sometimes faith comes in trusting the process and not telling someone what he or she should do. His body will tell him when he is ready. Lead him there. Stop fighting, even in your head. This is the real pattern that needs to be broken."

She returned to the family and to staff with this new path, and together they found moments of peace to guide them.

Cognitive psychologists teach that we cannot relinquish our beliefs unless we either whittle away at them for a very long time—usually years, with acceptable substitutions at the ready—or respond to an immense, even traumatic event that slices to the foundation these beliefs stand upon.[30]

We repeatedly entertain new possibilities, even as our historic views rush to reclaim their throne. It can feel like tides on a tumultuous sea.

Yet this is the soul's journey as we traverse the persistent pulse of hearts opening, growing, composting, and blooming. The river is always following itself home.

To befriend a soul, most especially in death, we lean into the current and nourish the journey. Perhaps this is the true nature of compassion—we release anything within us that might prevent us from doing so. We invite one another into the spaces and trust.

Compassion becomes "the continuous birth of creativity within and between us."[31] It is as powerful as death in its capacity for revelatory transformation.

❀   ❀   ❀

A FOSTER MOTHER, who had cared for a special needs child since birth, sat beside the little girl she loved as her own daughter as she slipped into the coma of death. For nearly ten years, she'd comforted her and miraculously nursed her back to health after multiple surgeries and treatments for a congenital condition now resistant to any further cure. The little girl, no bigger than a five-year-old, despite her age, had escaped death so many times that her mother kept looking for that hidden sign or miracle that would lead to recovery.

She continued to spoon cereal into her mouth, only to watch it spill down her chin. Gave her liquid vitamins for strength, saying, "She looks like a doll, her cheeks pink like this, how could she possibly be dying?"

The nurse and I sat with her while she cried and pointed out all the signs of life, even after staff had patiently taught her the signs of dying.

I'd never told a client my personal story, honoring the professional boundaries of my training, but this time, I couldn't see any other way to communicate besides one mother to another.

"The mind wants to believe anything else it can," I told her. "Anything."

"How do you know?" she asked. "How do you know when it's time to stop trying?"

I told her about the death of my daughter, Maggie, and the excruciating choice of stopping all medical care when it became clear she was dying.

"I was in the hospital, still unsure what to do. I was sleeping and not sleeping, heavily medicated, while my ex-husband thumbed through a medical journal, trying to read the statistical possibilities.

"At one point, I seemed to slip into a kind of dream about

Carol, a friend who once worked with my ex-husband. Her daughter was diagnosed with leukemia at a very young age. They had tried everything, even traveling to China for alternative healing, looking for new solutions and possibilities.

"Her daughter died about a year before we moved to the west coast. She was only fourteen.

"In the dream, I saw Carol sitting with her daughter. Her husband and youngest daughter were there too. Her daughter was sleeping in a hospital bed, wearing the pink crocheted hat that had adorned her head at her funeral. I could hear her breathing and realized these were the last hours of her life.

"I hadn't been there, nor heard the story, but somehow, it rose in my mind's eye as if it were occurring anew.

"The room seemed to arise within a pink-tinted bubble as I offered a similar prayer to yours—how did she know?

"How did she know her daughter was dying?

"How did she know when to stop trying?

"As soon as I spoke the question, Carol looked directly at me, as if all the veils dissolved. She grew in size until we were face to face, her expression a kindness I don't think any other woman in the world could have offered.

"We remained like this until I nodded with understanding. She lowered her head as if to bow. I returned the acknowledgement. Carol returned to her daughter, and the dream dissolved.

"I woke up and said to Rob, 'Our daughter is dying.'

"We simply knew."

She began to cry. The nurse and I did too.

Then I took her hand and invited her to look at her daughter with me.

"What do you see in her face?"

She could still see the rosy glow of her cheeks, but now noticed the beads of sweat, which in the sunlight made her look like an animated doll.

She noted the flutter of her eyelids, the heart shape of her mouth as she caught each breath, the soft bubbles of fluid, the rhythm, the growing pauses, the hiccup of her shoulders with each release.

She caressed the discoloration of her hands and feet, kissed toes and fingertips, and this time didn't try to explain away the symptoms. She knew too.

"She won't be here much longer," she finally whispered.

Love took over. She already knew what to do.

"Thank you," she said later. "I loved her to the end. Thank you."

She'd given all she could as a mother. This held her through the many months of sorrow and grief.

SHOWING UP

A supervisor once said, "We have not been asked to change people."

"Isn't change inherent in the request for our presence?" I asked.

"Change is inherent in the care we offer. Let go of your need to change things. Let people surprise you."

Sure enough, people have surprised me again and again, for deep below the surface of any crisis an endless reserve of love waits for the right conditions in which to flourish.

A Tibetan lama once said, "Love is the only protection we'll ever need."[32]

Paul said it differently when he taught the Corinthian community that love never fails, citing all the ways our other efforts fade away.[33]

It takes profound strength to sit with the dying, for we must remain steady and constant for long periods of unadorned silence while loved ones traverse the valley. We wait more often than we act.

This doesn't feel very natural in these modern times, as we are accustomed to filling all the empty spaces with another task or project. We have a tendency to search for solace in our distractions.

It still surprises me how many people do legal paperwork, watch television, rush off to clean the house, tuck in a few more hours of work, take another phone call, surf the internet, or even pack boxes rather than sit quietly with their loved one. We feel uncomfortable with the intensities death draws to the surface.

Perhaps this is why the sages of every tradition speak to the necessity of love, because when we shed the layered stories, relinquish all the effort, extinguish all the distractions, nothing else remains. This is the wisdom that compassion reveals.

To place our minds here first gives us the strength to face all else. Love leads us to give what is ours to give. This is the miracle. We just need to show up the best we can.

❋　❋　❋

WHEN I MET THE CEO of an international company, he was walking around the living room with a headset, dictating to his secretary.

Describing his meeting, Don laughed saying, "It's my company. I'm trying to make sure they know this. I've chosen my successor and written all our long-term policies. I will make sure they do what I wish for the next thirty years."

I nodded as he asked about my role on the hospice team.

"Wait until the boys hear I had a chaplain in the house. They'll never believe it."

We talked casually about his cancer, his life, all that he'd built in his career, and how he'd managed to play nine holes of golf that morning despite his rapid decline. Then he said, "I'm going to fight to the end. You watch. I won't stop fighting."

"Is this your philosophy about life?"

"It's how I got where I am today," he chuckled, almost mocking me as though I represented weakness in all its stereotypical forms, everything he'd stomped upon and beaten for thirty years.

"Well," I replied. "It's been my experience that when someone says they're going to fight, they do."

"You're damn right!"

"Then my suggestion is that you examine this a little further, for the best business deal requires knowing what the battle is about."

"I don't want to die. I will fight death until the bitter end."

"Sometimes we must fight for something rather than against something. Without this wisdom everything is an uphill struggle. We give away so much of our lives to war."

Within minutes, Don became too fatigued to talk. I did not see him again until his final hours, after the nurse called saying, "This is the worst terminal agitation I've ever seen."

Nothing consoled the anxiety, pain, shouting, and thrashing. When I arrived, the nurse was reviewing all the interventions with the family, listening for some missing piece of information that could turn the tide. I chose to sit with Don so they could continue to sort out a very difficult night.

I began to commingle my breath with his as he struggled, thinking, "Well, here we are..."

As if he heard my thoughts, Don suddenly turned and stared at me with what I could only call a fit of rage that lasted for a single breath cycle before dissolving into the query of raised eyebrows and a sigh, as if he suddenly remembered our first conversation. I reached out to him on the next inhalation, inviting him into the rhythms with each exhalation, until he began to follow like a drowning man grabbing a lifeboat.

I began to guide him, whispering, "That's right...good... that's right..." as each breath slowed, becoming further and further apart, until I knew his passing was imminent.

Then I made a tough decision. A few more minutes of shared breath and Don would release—it would be over. Yet I could hear his wife and son weeping in the foyer, exhausted from an all-night vigil in which they'd done the best they could. I didn't know if I should help him die or risk inviting his family to join us. I decided the family had the right to choose and alerted the nurse. The family rushed to join us.

We lost all ground as Don became violently agitated, practically screaming with frustration while his family stood helplessly beside him.

After another hour, unable to lead him back to the solace of breath, I invited his wife outside, hoping to teach her the breath practice so we could all work together. She couldn't stop crying from exhaustion and despair.

"I just want the best for him. But everyone is yelling at me, 'Do this. Don't do that!' I am scared and confused and want to run away, except that I promised him I'd be there. I just don't know if I can handle another hour of this."

"You can and you will," I stated, startling her.

"What?" she replied.

"This isn't about you anymore. It's about him, and he needs you. Love is never about whether or not things go well. It is about showing up. Let's talk about how you can show up."

I taught her simple mindfulness meditation.

"Watch his inhalation. Watch his exhalation. Concentrate only on this. Release every other thought. Stay present to your husband's experience. This is how to love him now."

We practiced together as she watched my chest rise and fall, rise and fall.

Suddenly, out of nowhere, she exclaimed, "Oh my god, this whole time I've only been thinking about myself. How I'm going to handle the children. How I'm going to handle his pain. How I'm going to handle my life after he dies. How I'm..."

She seemed to laugh and cry at once with her discovery.

"Christ only asked us to love our neighbors as our self. He

didn't ask us to change the world, only to see it through these eyes," I offered.

"I haven't been to church in years...but I can see Christ's face. Is that crazy?"

I shook my head, "No."

"Will you pray with me?"

"Of course."

When we finished, she beamed like a new bride.

"I love him. I will give him absolutely everything he needs until the end, no matter how hard it is."

Then she confessed, "I've been fighting with his daughter regarding the estate. We haven't spoken in weeks. She doesn't know he is dying."

She gave me permission to call her. When I held the phone up to Don's ear, he became completely still, clearly listening to every word his daughter spoke, mouthing the words goodbye, which we relayed to her.

Meanwhile, she taught her stepson about love. When he asked me how to commingle breath, I taught him too.

As they settled deeper into vigil, I went upstairs and made sandwiches, for no one had eaten in hours.

When I returned Don was wearing headphones.

"He loves his CDs of nature music. I don't know why I didn't think of it before. Look! He really likes the sounds. He seems calmer, don't you think?"

I nodded that indeed he did.

He died the following day, surrounded by his entire family.

A few weeks later she called, saying that she'd begun to attend church again, had renegotiated the will with her stepchildren, and had even shared lunch with both of them one day.

"I had no idea of the power of love," she told me. "Everywhere

I look I see people in need, and I help them. I have money, so I give it. And you know what? I miss him terribly, but I don't feel as lonely as I expected. I think he would be proud of me."

"I'm quite sure of it," I told her. "I think perhaps all that fighting masked a very gentle heart."

"Thank you. You gave me the gift of love just when I thought I was losing it."

NOT ALONE

There is a subtle play between solitude and intimacy—we must walk our path alone, but can do so within the kindness of fellow travelers. We learn how to share our lives while honoring the confidentialities of any heart.

A minister friend explained it like a mandala.

In our outer lives, we engage a world of strangers and new acquaintances with boundaries that regulate how much of our hearts we share with the public.

In our inner lives, we share friendships held together by the common values of community, work, and place. We negotiate boundaries that serve the group, yet have the individual freedom to come and go from some or all of these relationships as needed.

In our innermost lives, we share relationships with close intimates, opening our hearts fully to all the tended and untended feelings, our unsettled inquiries, our vulnerabilities as well as our strengths. We hold similar intentions, and support one another on both our personal and shared journeys.

In our secret lives, we enter the fullness of our hearts where all boundaries dissolve. We are simply present. We wordlessly commune with all life as we recognize the shared ground of being.

As we traverse our lives, we move in and out of these intima-

cies, sometimes focused upon one or another according to our circumstances, interdependent with all that our souls seek to explore. We live within the delicate balance of fluidity and need.

Yet, as we die, it is quite common for us to move away from all our outer connections to enter the inner, innermost, and secret places as we navigate the deep interiors of our own hearts. Even the most extroverted among us will relinquish all the ties once held in place by daily life, involuting into the boundaryless places, like a hermit entering retreat.

For some of us, this process can bring great fear or pain as we grieve the separations with our loved ones and engage our histories of being alone or lonely. For others, it is an immediate path of peace. This is as true for caregivers as it is for the dying.

We can feel like little children, unsure if we'll be alright. We can fight like children too, refusing all comfort except our own self-soothing. We return to the foundations of love that are wired into the hidden corridors of our psyche, engaging those early lessons of kindness and trauma. Forgotten secrets flush to the forefront as we seek love, acknowledgment, resolution, comfort, even power and control.

It is a fragile dance in which we play along that invisible edge between inner and outer. All the webs of connection respond to the mere whisper of change.

When I was a child, a Sunday school teacher taught, "Love covers a multitude of sins." Too young to understand most of what she said, I thought, "Love is more powerful than hurt."

Around the deathbed, this is a beautiful place to begin.

We hold a space large enough for anything and everything that arises within any heart—between any heart. We tenderly hold the string of connection the way we might hold a kite or a balloon, infuse it with the blessings of love, and when the time comes, release it.

Perhaps, in this simple act we can enter the timeless spaces, release

all boundaries, and recognize one another within the perfection of
existence, not just our capacity to relate.

❋   ❋   ❋

DIANE CARED FOR A dying neighbor who had no other
living friends or family. They'd slowly become friends after they
repeatedly ran into one another in the hallway of their apartment complex. For years they'd merely say hello, until Diane
began dropping off pies, flowers, and other gifts. Sophie would
receive the offering, but refuse any invitations into a more intimate relationship. She did the same with everyone.

Diane had become Sophie's power of attorney for health-
care when no one else could be found. She ensured that all
Sophie's needs were met, even staying in her apartment when
Sophie could no longer care for herself.

When the nurse suggested I visit Sophie, Diane agreed.

"It's so sad," Diane said. "You'd think the war would have
made her want people around. But I guess she lost too much.
She's a holocaust survivor, you know."

I nodded.

"The only reason you can visit is because she can't tell you
not to. She needs something I don't have to give. No one should
have to suffer alone like this."

I told her I'd do my best.

I'd visited many survivors of war, but no one could have
prepared me for the numbers branded onto her wrist. I felt as if
I had stepped into her private cell of childhood horror.

As soon as she saw me, she leapt up in the bed and began
screaming, pulling her hair, scratching at her flesh, throwing
pillows, grabbing covers. Her eyes were glazed over and red. I
don't know how anyone had managed to get near her to offer

even the simplest of care. I sat in a chair as far away from the bed as possible, so I wouldn't disturb her further.

She eyed me carefully, and I remained as still as possible, not even daring to join her breath. I simply tried to give her time to become comfortable with my presence in the room.

She quickly dismissed me, returning to what felt like a remembered war as she sat up, laid down, and circled the bed on all fours. She did this ritually, again and again, when suddenly she leapt toward the end of the bed snarling. She threw her body against an invisible threat, as if trying to stop a pouncing tiger, then, just as quickly, recoiled as if slapped.

She crawled back to the wall, clutched the headboard, and pulled herself up, poised for the next attack.

In the momentary pause, I glimpsed a hallmark card perched on the nightstand on the other side of the bed—the only personal item in a room she'd inhabited for twenty years. On the cover was a colorful image of an angel hanging from a falling star, like a gleeful gymnast. Red glitter filled most of the surrounding spaces with whimsy.

Her ritual began again as she circled, lunged, retreated, when suddenly, she hesitated in the middle of the bed and looked up at the ceiling.

I took a chance.

"We are not alone even when we're alone."

She glared at me as though she'd become the tiger, causing me to grab the edges of my chair. Yet something stirred in her eyes, encouraging me to continue.

"Sometimes love hangs from a star, wearing a purple dress with gold trim, smiling at us."

I held her gaze without stirring.

"Sometimes love hangs from a star..."

She leaned against the headboard, still watching me. Then she looked up again.

"Sometimes we just have to look for the star."

She craned her neck as if looking at the sky on a clear night, then looked back at me, the sky, me, and laid down.

I covered her with a blanket I found on the floor, stroked her back, and hummed a simple lullaby as she fell asleep.

RADICAL KINDNESS

Home health aides and hospice nurses talk about pedicures, changing sheets, and washing hair as though they were the most ordinary of tasks. They laugh and joke about the latest shampoos, basins, and clippers, interwoven with details of wound care and the movement of bowels.

One time, I arrived early for an appointment to find a trusted friend and colleague washing the feet of a patient who could no longer sit up unassisted. He spent his days watching birds at the feeder his son had hung near the window, dependent upon the kindness of others for his most basic needs.

She used her bare hands to clean his feet and ankles, careful not to tear his fragile skin. Then she patted them dry, covered them with oil, and pulled on a pair of fleece socks to keep him warm.

She sang while she washed, holding a towel to his mouth when he coughed. Sometimes he'd laugh or ask a question, but mostly, he'd close his eyes and receive.

When she left, he and I sat quietly together for thirty minutes, watching the sparrows, neither of us initiating a conversation. There wasn't anything else to do.

In the quiet, I remembered a conversation I'd shared with a former Catholic nun. We'd taken a walk across the grounds of a Benedictine convent, where we were attending a weekend workshop.

An ardent follower of Dorothea Day and Thomas Merton, she had studied the necessities of caring for the poor and broken among us, wondering if Jesus had been crucified for his inclusive kindness, not merely for political or religious differences.

"He broke a lot of ecclesiastical rules in his few short years of teaching," she commented. "One of them was his inclusion of women. Some of us feel that this social activity was what got him into trouble with the reigning hierarchies. Theological differences can be argued and forgiven. Popularity, however, causes problems."

She laughed.

"He really did follow a radical path of compassion!"

I agreed.

"Yet I've never been able to figure out why it is so dangerous to love a woman, or worse, be loved by one," she added.

She'd married shortly after leaving the convent and chose not to have children, as her life was full of community and social action shared with her husband. They coordinated a homeless shelter, organized an interfaith gathering of prayer that met at their house each week, collected clothing for the women's shelter where she volunteered her services as a spiritual director, and once a week drove people from her church to doctors appointments when they could no longer afford a taxi fare.

"We are called to acts of humble love in every hour. This is the simplicity. Jesus bent down and washed the feet of every single disciple, understanding that one leads by following," she told me. "He'd already surrendered to God. He had nothing left to lose."

She laughed again.

"That's what made him so dangerous. He followed the laws of God, of love, and on that day, he behaved like a woman, for it's unlikely that men of that era ever touched the feet of another.

"He knelt before his friends and recklessly gave away the power

his leadership afforded him. He greeted his friends like a woman,
through the kindness of touch.

"Something, don't you think?"

As I considered the kindness of my friend washing the feet of a
man she barely knew, I thought so too.

☼   ☼   ☼

WHEN I MET CURTIS, he'd been living for more than a
decade in a two-room house with his mother. The cabin sat
on a small creek, deep in the wilderness, and was built by his
parents when they first moved to California. His mother was
diagnosed with Alzheimer's shortly after his father died. Curtis had chosen to move in with her so he could attend her needs
rather than place her in a nearby facility.

He lived as a hermit, denying himself the typical paths of
happiness expected for a man in his mid-fifties.

At the office, we secretly confessed to one another that each
of us had silently assessed his mental health, worried that perhaps he had ulterior motives for living alone with his mother,
something I doubt any of us would have considered had he
been a woman.

Yet all of us concurred that Curtis was a man of the highest
ethics, for he often stated, "If I cannot love my own mother,
what good would a job be to me? She gave me life, and now I
care for hers."

He chose to live according to his beliefs.

Each day, he hauled water from the nearby well, cooked
elaborate meals from the garden, attended each bodily need,
mended fences, and maintained all the tools and machinery.

Curtis spoke like a monk in slow rhythmical patterns that

held more space than words, as though he heard silence within every sound. His mom chuckled each time he spoke, like a woman cooing to a newborn infant cradled in her arms. The two of them laughed together, seemingly all the time.

One day we talked about meditation. Curtis asked if there was a difference between prayer and observing the details of someone or something you love.

I laughed saying, "I doubt there is much difference."

"This morning I brought my mom a sunflower. She held it for more than an hour, repeating, 'It's so beautiful.'"

"My son did that with a sunflower when he was four."

"Really?"

"He pulled up a chair next to the flower and stared into its center just like your mom. He sat there for thirty minutes. When I asked him about it, he smiled saying, 'It's just so beautiful, mom.'"

Curtis smiled. "Funny how the world changes when you look at it through someone else's eyes. I just wanted to give her a gift, and now I'm the humble one, looking for the beauty in a flower."

I told him the story of the Buddha who, at the start of a teaching, held a flower in front of him while hundreds of followers tried to figure out what he meant. Yet one man in the front row, Mahakasyapa, simply gazed into the flower and smiled.

"Yes!" he exclaimed. "It's like that. My mom sees something. If I simply pay attention to her, care for her, love her, I see it too."

PRESENCE

I can scarcely speak of all the times staff and I have sat with a patient everyone else abandoned.

"You don't have to stay," a nurse told me once. "You're a chaplain. You don't have to see this. It's okay if you want to walk away."

"If I am unable to look into the suffering, where will the solace come from?" I replied.

People who enter hospice sometimes feel abandoned, as if everyone has given up on them and simply sent them home to die. I think it might come from the commonly used phrase, "There's nothing more we can do."

Healthcare professionals use this phrase to announce the end of curative possibilities. They let the lack of medical options lead into a conversation about death.

Yet it can feel traumatic to face death in this way. The words cut through all the hopes and fears with an unwelcome fury. We react with anger, blame, shame, or despair. Hospice can become a mark of failure, or worse, exile from the world of living.

I don't have solutions for a bulging healthcare system, as families are pressed to the edges of all their resources, unsure how to find enough time or money to handle the crisis. Nor do I have easy answers for the ethical issues our aging culture faces.

Yet every single wisdom tradition in the world knows what to do within the box of impossible. We all do.

Love. Be kind. Be with.

Once, a friend and colleague came to a weekend workshop where I was teaching about spiritual pain. He asked clear questions about how to help someone in a coma, as he wasn't sure if "anyone was in there anymore."

I gave as many examples as possible to describe the nature of soulness, using stories from my work to introduce each complex truth, but he had no context within his own experience. He couldn't understand the teachings.

About two hours after we finished, I received a call that he'd had a stroke and was in the hospital, unable to speak. When I walked into his room, tears ran down his cheeks. I simply held his hand, saying, "It's okay. I'm here, whether I understand what you're saying or not."

He spent the next several days receiving tests and evaluations as doctors skillfully searched for causes and the appropriate treatment. Regardless, his nights were filled with anxiety, caused not only by the stroke but also by his inability to communicate.

One night, a nurse walked past his room, heard him crying, and sat with him as he wept. She listened as he grasped at inaccessible words. Unlike so many others, she didn't guess what he was saying, or try to piece the words together, or offer any advice, recommendations, or clichés. For nearly an hour, she simply gazed into his eyes, offering space for his being-ness, as well as his process, until he collapsed into tears and stopped trying to speak, falling into a peace that never left him.

The next day his symptoms started to shift. He could move his hand, and words began to return. Although we could all point toward skillful medical care, he felt the healing began with the kindness of a woman who took the time to sit with him as he wrestled with the immensity of his questions.

"I felt as if God dwelled in her and that this God I'd never spoken

with reached out to touch me in the heart of my despair. It's as if this kindness is everywhere now, and we're part of it. You know?"

When he returned to work a few months later, he offered the same kindness to his patients. He listened and waited before offering solutions, trusting they would be revealed within the exchange of kindness.

"I am not the same. I don't think my patients are either."

※　※　※

IT WAS A WARM SUMMER DAY when I climbed the stairs of an apartment complex to meet Helen, a woman in her late twenties, who was dying of end-stage liver disease. She couldn't remember a time in which she didn't drink; her childhood memories were consumed by the side effects of a disease that began in junior high school. She'd tried innumerable outpatient and inpatient treatments to no avail.

Helen confessed that she didn't know which was worse, the anxiety of sobriety or the hangover after a weekend binge.

"When I drink, for a little while I am unconscious. It is the only rest I know."

She and I sought other sources of rest while her social worker supported her addiction treatments. Regardless, one Friday night Helen went on a binge, and this time her body simply quit.

I visited despite warnings of what I'd find.

"There is nothing more you can do for her."

"I know."

Her mother met me at the door and led me to the living room. As we talked, she folded towels she'd used to absorb the persistent hemorrhaging. Another load spun in the washer.

Hour after hour, she bathed her daughter, cleaned up the discharge, did the laundry, and began again.

We entered her daughter's bedroom together.

The room was quiet, with no sound but Helen's raspy snores. The sun streamed through a closed window onto a sparkling clean room that smelled of baby wipes and dryer sheets. It felt like a nursery.

Helen nearly filled her full-sized bed as stagnant fluids filled every swollen cell of her body. I didn't recognize her.

I tried to connect in all the prayerful ways I knew, but she was completely unresponsive. Her mom and I simply sat together holding hands. There wasn't anything else to do.

On the way home, I called a friend. I could find no words for the futility, the loss, the suffering. I simply wept.

I visited for three more days.

Each time, her mom welcomed me warmly. We'd sit on the couch together for a few minutes, reassuring me she was alright, and then we'd visit Helen together. I'd offer a few prayers, and we'd return to silent watching and waiting.

Then, I'd drive home, still unsettled, still crying.

Back at the office I asked the home health aide, who visited daily as well, "How do you do it?"

"When I wash her face, I imagine Christ. When I wash her feet, I imagine Mary doing the same. Then, after a little while, the imaginings disappear, and I don't know...I guess, I just love her. Her body. The humility of life."

On my final visit, I brought anointing oils.

"Do you think she'll notice?" asked her mom.

"I don't know, but we will. Let's offer whatever peace we find as a gift to her."

"I'd like that."

RADIANCE

As a trained psychotherapist, I am accustomed to assessing problems, or at the very least, devising solutions. This is true for all my professional colleagues, nurses and doctors included.

Yet these skills dance differently around the deathbed. Solutions aimed at dying bodies and psyches can feel more like noise than help if our efforts resurrect the very things now releasing.

One time, a friend showed me an ink painting.

"A Rorschach game?"

"No," she laughed. "Look at the image. Let your mind pick out shapes, images, meaning."

"Okay. A woman. A man and a woman. Two heads. Twins. Joined at the hip. One morphing into another."

"Good. Now look at the spaces around the image. See the image, but stop looking at it."

I laughed. "Okay."

I had a difficult time turning away from the construct, the artistic object. My mind kept probing, searching, cataloguing. I turned away, tried again, and then I got it. I simply gazed at the beauty without trying to find anything.

"Now what do you see?"

"A butterfly. How is that possible?"

"Because your mind stopped looking at a thing and therefore,

stopped looking for your impression or interpretation. The true image can only be seen in the spaces when everything else (dies) disappears."

Perhaps this is the most important reason we look for the beauty. We look between the cracks of problems and solutions, for this is where the soul plays. We enter the humility of not knowing and taste the revelations now free to emerge.

❋ ❋ ❋

MARIA, AN ELDERLY WOMAN with Alzheimer's, lived in the same house where she'd raised five children. Her youngest daughter, Mia, had quit her job and moved in to care for her, while other siblings stayed weekends or during the week as they were able.

Maria frightened easily with strangers, sudden movements, or any change in routine by flailing, shouting, and crying until everything stabilized once more. It required round-the-clock care to keep her both calm and cared for.

Yet the biggest struggle was providing medical care. Maria had a large, necrotic wound on her thigh that was open to the bone and required regular attention. Every time a nurse stepped into the room she screamed, hurled pillows, kicked, scratched, and hid beneath covers in anticipation of painful procedures. No one could figure out exactly how she recognized nurses, even new ones, but her response was the same. All of us did what we could not to startle her.

The first time I visited, Mia had moved Maria to a hardback chair. She wore a simple cotton dress, a blanket across her lap, and sat with her ankles crossed, although they didn't touch the floor. She wrung her hands, chewed as if she had gum, and studied me like an unanswered question.

As Mia tucked the sheets and blankets into tight corners, she commented, "The priest still visits her every week. They are old friends..."

Suddenly, Maria began screaming for no known reason.

Without thinking, I began praying the rosary, gazing deeply into her eyes with each phrase. She calmed instantly, surprising us all.

"She's old school. She loves the rosary," Mia chuckled, stroking Maria's hair and face.

I began to make weekly visits to pray the rosary. I purposely left my bags, notebooks, or any other sign of hospice in the living room and entered with nothing more than a rosary around my wrist. With each recitation, Maria would take my hand between hers and pet each finger, knuckle, and palm as she listened.

One day, I overheard the nurse strategizing about her next visit. Maria's wound had worsened. She really needed treatment. Staff was trying to figure out how to get close enough to render care as it was too technical for family.

I offered to arrive first to recite the rosary in case this might help and called her daughter to tell her of our plan. She gave her permission, even though we weren't representatives of her church, for she'd "seen the delight of rosary visits and was up for anything that would help."

I arrived mid-morning, just as the sun broke through the winter clouds, and sat in the hardback chair beside her bed, reciting the familiar prayers as Maria watched. Meanwhile, the nurse memorized and practiced the words on her drive, arriving about fifteen minutes later.

As the nurse entered the room, she slipped into the recitations with me, our voices an immediate duet that caused Maria to smile. With this success, the nurse slowly crept toward the other side of the bed until Maria noticed and began her habitual resistance.

We increased the volume of prayer rather than try to distract or console her. The change seemed to create confusion, for she tipped her head and listened like a school teacher might. She waited, listened, paused, and then simply returned her gaze to me as if it were just the two of us like usual.

As we continued to chant, the nurse rearranged Maria's blankets and unwrapped the bandages. She cleaned, washed, clipped, and stitched as though they were a natural part of prayer. Our words seemed to find an easy rhythm with both the medical care and the subtle shifts of emotion, as if the words were comfort, invitation, invocation, and strength all at once.

Mia had been watching from the doorway, ready to help if needed. When she brought in a stack of clean towels, as the nurse tenderly finished her work, she added her voice to the song, resurrecting what felt like the most ancient of rituals.

A few days later, the nurse sent me a card: "Here was a woman with such a sick body, skin falling apart, but something beautiful shined from her that day, and I know it really is always in there somewhere. I'm reminded of Jesus touching the lepers when no one else would."

A few weeks later, Maria entered the dying process.

When her son opened the door to invite me in, I smelled roses rather than the smell of damp necrosis from the weeks before. I looked around the entire living room, the kitchen, but couldn't see a bouquet of flowers anywhere. As he led me toward her bedroom, the scent grew thicker, and still, there were no vases, no open windows onto a garden, no signs of roses anywhere.

I sat next to the bed holding rosary beads, looking for pressed flowers or any other explanation for the intense smell of roses. With each decade of the rosary, the scent intensified and her breath softened, dissolving into the shared rhythm of breath and prayer.

When I finished all the prayers, I sat with her in silent wonder. Her luminous face seemed fluid, color shifting through flesh as if she were a rainbow in the sky after a long rain. I felt bathed by a nondescript radiance that touched my inner core as if we sat beneath or even within the very same sunlight.

All bridges dissolved. She was the rosary. She was prayer. It bathed us all.

GRACE

"Behind most of the religious rituals of humanity we find the original impulse to bring more blessing and compassion into everyday life."[34]

We enter a transformative process meant to shed old skins so we can grow into a bigger view of both ourselves and the world. We call upon the energies living within the cellular structures of existence to help us do so.

However, many of us are shy about such prayer, if we go there at all. We are accustomed to traversing anything we might call the spiritual path within the capacity of our own independence. We are cautious about entering into conversations that could lead to the punctuation of religious differences or an argument about beliefs.

Yet it is in the simplicity of reaching beyond all we think we know that wisdom breaches our carefully laid plans, inviting us to receive what can only be tasted, not found. We cannot truly see the sky until we walk through the door. Grace opens the door so we can.

This is the lineage of kindness that awaits us. For any who slip past the boundaries, release the noose of separation, and merge into the radiant oneness of love become living invitations, arising again and again upon the current of life, tossing morsels of kindness in an infinite array to greet any request.

We simply need the right conditions to receive. More times than not, this is devotion. We love the guides, midwives, teachers, gurus, and deities who've gone before.

Of all the lessons I've learned around the deathbed, it's the effort-lessness that stands out. Perhaps it was my training or the years of wrestling with the self-denigration of grief, but I thought there would be so much to do, so much that needed to be done—the endless job of mitigating suffering.

Yet, more times than not, when I did my best work I became invisible, as though I disappeared into a flow of kindness that was never mine to begin with. In these places, I became like words that could point the way, but had to dissolve so someone could find their *way.*

What held me, what held all of us, was the simplicity inherent in remaining present to a force that already knew what to do. We evoked the presence of grace in as many languages as there were people. Then, we simply trusted the process.

A colleague once asked how I could pray with so many people in so many languages. "Aren't you lying when you pray to Jesus one minute and Tara the next?"

"This isn't about whether or not I believe, or even if I believe what someone else believes. I have been on my knees so lost I couldn't find my feet, much less walk. In such moments, prayer comes with an ease that forgets words or images and settles into a flow of tears that journey as far back as God's own longings. It doesn't matter what form or language grace speaks, only that it speaks. And that we listen."

❄   ❄   ❄

I ONCE VISITED A MOTHER whose twenty-five-year-old son, Thomas, was dying from a congenital disease. Most doctors had not expected him to live past infancy.

He had been bed-bound since birth, growing to the size of a school-aged boy before his body froze in time, each joint curling around the increasing stiffness. He looked like a withered, miniature oak tree.

She'd painstakingly cared for all his needs at home, alone, except for the help of immediate family, for the entirety of his life.

I visited with a coworker, who offered to translate, as English was the family's second language, but it turned out we could communicate well, and so it felt more like a gathering of friends.

Accustomed to medical professionals, the mother began with a report of his eating habits, sleeping patterns, and other daily routines, checking them against his history as if looking for subtle indications that could dismiss his need for hospice.

She'd talk, then pause, tending to his nonverbal cues as though we were on the periphery of their dyadic process. She caught every subtlety. With each response, he'd smile with newborn wonder. She'd whisper a few words, he'd smile, and then she'd seamlessly return to our conversation as though everything was embedded within their choreography of care.

During one of the pauses, I asked, "Who do you turn to when you feel afraid or tired?"

She told us about her family.

Her teenage daughter helped after school, though she'd become interested in boys, which caused frequent disagreements. Her husband worked two jobs, coming home to eat dinner and sleep, though more than once he risked his job to respond when she needed help. As a family, they managed what to many seemed impossible.

Then I asked, "Tell me about your heart strength," as my friend translated the subtleties of the question.

"I see the presence of Mary," I said, pointing to a photo on the wall above her son. *Presencia de María.* "How do you stay strong? What keeps you going?"

She offered her son a sip of water, sat down, paused, and then put her hand into her apron, pulling out a prayer card of Mary.

"She's beautiful," I replied.

The prayer card came from a small town where La Virgen de Guadalupe had visited a young girl in a dream. Spontaneous healings had been reported by local residents and visitors ever since.

She drove several hundred miles to the shrine where the apparition had occurred, when it became obvious that Thomas shared the same disease as his older brother, who died as a toddler. This was the first time any of us had heard about her eldest son.

She prayed to La Virgen for Thomas to live, promising she'd be faithful no matter what. The local priest offered her the card as a gift when he saw her weeping by the fountain as she cradled her toddler son across her lap.

As Thomas grew, his condition worsened, and when a visiting doctor told her about treatment options in America, she took this as a sign, a direct request from La Virgen de Guadalupe. Together with her husband, against all odds, they found a way to bring their family across the border.

She paused again, staring into the photo of La Virgen.

"I saw Her," she said, tears streaming down her face. "I saw Her."

I nodded as she carefully revealed the details of her vision.

Then she showed us another prayer card. This one was a gift from another holy site. When it came in the mail from an old friend, she had slipped it beneath the mattress of her son's bed.

She paused to wipe the spittle from around her son's mouth, covered his feet with a blanket, and tucked the photo back into her pocket.

"It takes strength for a mother to stand next to the cross while her son dies," I remarked.

"Yes." She smiled, "She will help me. She is always here."

GRATITUDE

As children, most of us learn to say thank you each time we receive a gift. We also sigh, thank you, when tragedy passes us over, grateful to escape anything we may fear.

Yet David Whyte teaches that real gratitude is the capacity to be awake in the presence of life as it courses both within and about us.[35] *We gaze into anything that arises to see the ineffable beauty rather than outcome.*

This is the path of all meditative and prayerful practice—to open our hearts to the possibility that we are what we sought all along.

"A moment will come when Divine pulsation grabs you and carries you into its dance," teaches the Vijnana Bhairava Tantra.[36]

Joy flows naturally as we play upon this current, surrendering into the pulse of our own origins. "This is the ceaseless throb, the rhythm of life—Terrifying in its eternity, exquisite in its constancy."[37]

Gratitude is another form of namaste *in which we wonder how this essential knowing sees, not merely what it sees. We gaze into the eyes of any phenomena with innocence, freed from the constraints of our own expectations.*

We won't do so immediately, for it is a practice born within our dance with grace. Perhaps this is why so many sages teach us to thank even our most painful experiences, for nothing exists apart from this dance.

Each time we gaze into anything we fear, especially death, it becomes a mirror. Gratitude invites us to see more than our own needs and desires.

❃ ❃ ❃

A FEW WEEKS AFTER Barbara died, her son Luke called. He'd returned to college, and sought support through a local grief group and on-campus counseling, but felt disappointed.

"I can't seem to get anybody to understand that something in me feels better. You were there. Am I crazy?"

In the final hours of her life, Barbara had become agitated, crying out for someone to help the children.

"Help the children," she'd cry. "Help the children! They are hungry!"

Then she'd wrestle with the covers tucked around her, desperately trying to climb out of bed to reach them.

"There are so many. They are brown and yellow and red and white and black, and they are hungry. I don't know how to feed them. How do I feed them all?"

Her siblings tried to convince her that her children were fine, but their consolations seemed to intensify her agitation.

When I arrived, they took a needed break, so Luke and I could sit with her.

I'd met with Barbara for more than nine months. Diagnosed with brain cancer, she experienced very few side effects until the final few weeks of her life. This gave us time to share long conversations about her work, her family, her beliefs, and her relationship with a Divinity she saw in every human being.

She'd been an elementary school teacher who often brought food from home for the children whose families didn't have enough money for breakfast. "Sometimes, it was the only food they had besides the subsidized lunches," she'd observed.

She was also a Christian woman who'd spent years questioning the interface of God and suffering. She never understood why we couldn't put aside our religious differences, roll up our sleeves, and serve one another.

"This is the message, I think," she said one morning. "Not all our theories about why God lets bad things happen, because they do happen, all the time.

"I've wondered if that's why we're here—to love one another like God loves us, for we are all God's children. Maybe this is the entire plan?"

As I watched her reach out to hungry children Luke and I couldn't see, I wondered if her search for God had transformed into a need to feed all the children. I wondered if it had become the singularity of love.

Breathing with the rhythms of intermittent rest and struggle, I waited for a natural pause, hoping she'd come close to the edge of the bed so I could speak to her with the least amount of disturbance.

When the moment came, I paraphrased Christ's words: "God loves the children too."

She seemed to hear me clearly, concentrating upon my face as if to remember who I was, perhaps even our conversations, though I really couldn't be sure.

"Come to me as little children," I offered, pausing once more.

The panic seemed to recede from her face, and so I suggested, "Let's take the children to Jesus."

Her breathing slowed. She looked at the ceiling, out the window, toward an unseen vision at the end of her bed, gripping the bed railing as if to leap.

"Christ sits upon a grassy hillside. A few wildflowers still bloom. The sun shines upon the sea below," I imagined aloud, invoking a story from the gospels.

"There is bread, fish, jugs of water.

"And children. One, two, dozens, hundreds."

"Yellow, black, red, white, brown," she added.

"Yes."

"Tommy, Jose, Darlene, Susan…"

"Yes, bring them all."

She continued to gather the children, "Mary, John, Lucinda, Noel…"

On the next pause, I asked, "Are you there too? Are you with the children?"

She replied, "We are all children?"

"Yes."

"God loves all the children," she sighed.

"Yes, God cares for all the children. Go to Jesus, and the children will be cared for."

She sat up in the bed and became perfectly still, like a meditator in a cave.

More time passed in pregnant silence.

Then she looked directly at me.

"I have them," she said. "They are here. We are all here."

Then she giggled, "Yes, we have them."

She laid back onto her pillow, repeating as she fell asleep, "We have them. The children are safe. Oh, the beautiful children are safe."

As Luke recalled these events, checking his memory with mine, he said, "All those years of church and no one told me anything like this. I don't know what to do with it.

"It's like I can see what my mom did, and now I want to

do something different. I feel confused, unsure, and strangely ashamed because I don't want to be a religious fanatic."

We talked about prayer, meditation, and a variety of spiritual traditions, focusing on the essential support he was seeking rather than the seemingly enormous array of religious possibilities. I gave him some questions to ask possible teachers and group leaders.

A month later, he told me he'd found a Christian meditation group that honored both eastern and western sensibilities as they explored a contemplative prayer practice in which one listens and then rests in the silence. He was able to honor his mom's heritage while staying true to the meditative proclivities he found in himself.

"And the strange thing is that when I made space for what happened during my mom's death, I found room to miss her too. I'm really sad that we never found a way to talk about God. She was always trying to convert me. I hope she knows I heard her this time."

GIVE AWAY

Recently, a friend and I talked about the nature of stars, the qualities of soil, and the cycles of weather.

"We are made of material that is billions of years old," she said. "We are billions of years old."

As a painter, she layers color atop color to create images with the radiant depth of contrast and synergy, while others appear from the unplanned merging of pigments. In one moment, we can see a human being dancing across the oceanic sky. Then a face peers through golden clouds tunneling through a palette of stones. A treasure box spills jewels in the corner where she signs her name.

"Maybe it really is a play?" we mused.

Every year, my birthday falls at the peak of the Perseid showers, a display of shooting stars caused when the Earth passes through a ring of meteoric fragments. I invite friends over, and we throw blankets on the ground to watch the fireworks that I jokingly claim as my own private, sky party.

This year, as I reach another one of those milestone years that delineate the inevitability of aging, I find myself contemplating how stars only shine when everything else has been given away.

We offer our greatest light in that final dance across the sky.

I can still remember the scent of every soul whose death I witnessed, even as their names recede into history. They are living memories of perfection, freed of all other conditions.

This is the beauty—death reveals what can only be seen in a naked sky.

※　　※　　※

AFTER READING A dense psychological history of my client, I passed through several locked check stations before arriving at the ward he'd lived in for thirty years. The courts deemed him too medically ill to stand trial for the crimes he committed.

"I have spent all these years learning not to listen to hallucinations," he began when I introduced myself as a hospice chaplain. "The psychiatrist told me to practice seeing something before I believe it. I don't see cancer, so how do I know if the doctor is telling me the truth?"

Nurses, psychiatrists, oncologists, and trusted staff members had repeatedly shown him x-ray images, MRI scans, specialized reports.

"How do I know those are mine? What are those blobs anyway? Are they from inside me or from a building down the street? What do they mean anyway?"

"They explain why you are on hospice."

"Yeah, they say I'm dying."

I nodded.

"I can't see death, either."

We both laughed at the sudden absurdity.

"Do you believe you'll die one day?" I asked him.

He rolled a cigarette between his fingers as he examined the dirt beneath his thumbnail, then looked out the window at a blossoming walnut tree. He nodded toward a couple of friends, waved at one, and then checked to ensure no one was listening before whispering, "Yes. Even God died on the cross. I guess I must too."

He never asked about cancer again. Our conversations became philosophical instead.

"How should I pray when everything is so unpredictable?

"Will God win the war of good and evil?

"How do I offer forgiveness to someone who won't listen?

"What if time runs out, and there's unresolved anger with friends or family?"

Then he'd conclude, "I'm going to die. I can live with that. I can live with that."

One day, I arrived as the symptoms became more pronounced. He felt too tired to step outside the facility to smoke cigarettes.

"I'm exhausted. I think something's eating me up. Is this cancer?"

"Yes. This is how cancer behaves."

He nodded with a studied acceptance.

"I wish I could still go outside. I can't talk to my friends anymore." He paused and then laughed saying, "I give a lot of advice."

Over the years, the gatherings in the courtyard had become informal support groups. He'd been there the longest, so naturally, others turned to him for advice. They spoke freely, sometimes processing therapy groups, and sometimes talking about memories, regrets, or sorrows they felt uncomfortable sharing in formal settings.

"They ask me church questions," he said. "They're afraid of priests and want to know about what I've seen, what I've read, what to believe in, but mostly, they just want to confess, hoping this will save them. Some of them can get real scared. Do you think there's a way for me to join them again?"

"What does your body say?" I replied.

"I'm too tired. It's time for me to spend my days indoors."

"Have you heard of Thomas Merton?"

He nodded.

"He spent much of his adult life arguing with his superiors for a monk's cell so he could live a life of prayer and contemplation," I recalled. "They wanted him to be part of the world, and he wanted to embrace the world with his prayers."

"I've prayed all my life," he confessed, "even when my mind succumbed to untruths. I hurt people then. I am here so I won't hurt anyone else. Now I can no longer help anyone here either."

He told me he'd wanted to be a priest when he was a child, and so I asked, "What if you imagined this room and this bed as the cell of a monk?"

"You mean to pray?"

"Yes," I replied. "Thomas Merton taught that we go to prayer when we discover there is nowhere else to go. Until then, we tend to get lost in the cycles of chaos and happiness until something pierces our hearts so deeply we seek mercy.

"Then we get tired of fighting, and this reveals the truth of our fight—one day we will lose everything we try to hold onto.

"Death hovers beneath every fear.

"Within this realization, we pray to open—to give it all away rather than lose it. We find comfort within the harrowing need."[38]

"I know what that feels like," he said. "I have felt that kind of afraid before. I did many terrible things. I made others afraid too."

"Did prayer help?"

"Yes. Even before I believed anything."

"Perhaps you've been given permission to be a monk for a little while."

"I'd like to think that even in my last days I could offer comfort to someone else. I will pray for my friends."

From then on, those of us who visited him wondered what mental illness really means, for as one of the nurses said, "He's saner than most of my friends."

We'd enter. He'd smile, hold our hands, and gaze into our eyes until everything seemed to melt into love. Then he'd close his eyes and rest.

It was as if he had nothing else to do.

More than one of us wished to know such peace.

PARTICIPATION

The island where I live is a unique confluence of rocky contours and a sea tamed by a bowl of mountains whose roots run beneath the water like an underground city. Birds traverse the archipelago every season, some flying north, some south, passing all the locals regardless of which direction they travel.

A pair of bald eagles lives up the road in a nest built long before I moved here. They chat like songbirds before flying so low across the landscape their shadows temporarily make me feel like a mouse.

Ravens live deep in the forest, venturing out mid-morning to see what survived the night and to look for offerings I might have made. Hummingbirds startle me as they dart across the porch, thrilled by early spring blossoms and an abundance of flowering plum and apple trees.

Geese squawk day and night, as hawks, dogs, minks, and otters threaten their cache of eggs. Frogs belch. Swallows flit over a nearby pond where the deer will visit come sunset. Redwing blackbirds coo to potential mates.

I've watched these comings and goings for years now. Yet, no matter how many guidebooks I read, I still can't find those telltale signs that cause birds to leave one home for another with a migratory precision that times their arrival with the first blooming tulip, despite the preceding weeks of snow and rain. Some of it baffles scientists too, and I wonder if all of us are like beachcombers searching for secrets in the shifting sands.

Yet, most of the time, this precise symbiosis of needs and drives feels more like a symphony than an unanswered question. The song curls around the hills of wildflowers and cedar trees, dips into a nearby creek, and swirls into the house like a gentle breeze. I check the flowers, drink tea, listen, and begin my day.

Each of us is filled with longings, memories, gifts, and stories. We have strengths, limitations, visions, and blind spots that connect us to a choir that has only ever needed our voice. Regardless of our trajectories—the plans, the successes and failures, the trails we did or didn't travel—we were never the entire song. In this we cannot fail, only play.

I wish I could say this to anyone sitting on the edge of the bed, wringing out her life against the maws of finitude.

We never had much time, for it is within this boundary we exist. Our contribution is part of the evolutionary wonder of rolling tides upon a vast ocean.

We belong. We have always belonged.

SOON AFTER I MOVED to my new home, I was invited to a Passover dinner at a local restaurant. It was a private affair, and we sat on either side of long wooden tables covered with white linens and a few sprigs of rosemary and lavender.

The reader would lead us step-by-step through the Old Testament story of Passover, followed by songs sung by a canter in Hebrew. When he sat down, the servers would bring the next course of food. Then we'd eat and talk with one another.

It didn't take very long before strangers became friends, huddled around the table contemplating life and death.

"We seek the life of the mind," said one man, a professor at a nearby table.

"We seek love," said a woman with eight grandchildren.

"We seek good food," laughed another, as we concurred that the chicken soup was possibly the best we'd ever tasted.

I felt part of the community, the land, tradition, for no one had ever connected so many aspects of life together within a sensuality of delight tasted by us all.

Our differences faded. Time stopped. Ritual carried us into the cave of hope and fear. We asked new questions.

A few years later, I received a call from a woman named Patricia, inviting me to visit when she discovered her husband, Paul, would soon die. She'd been raised in a Protestant Christian tradition, while her husband had grown up Jewish. She didn't know how to address the disparities now that death knocked at their door.

They'd never talked much about religion because they both had grown children when they met, and they simply respected one another's individual paths. As his family brought new ritual into the house, she felt confused, even alienated, unsure of what to do.

A large photograph of Jerusalem hung on the wall behind her as we spoke. They'd visited Israel together, traveling to both the Western Wall as well as the Church of the Sepulchre, even walking past the Temple Mount, noting the physical proximity of sacred sites from three great traditions so frequently in conflict. They bought the photograph as a symbol of their marriage—the possibility of peacemaking.

The rabbi arrived as we shared tea. After a few niceties, he invited us to join him around the bedside as he offered prayers for Paul.

We wound down the stairs through a brief tunnel of white stucco walls, into a daylight basement with large windows overlooking the valley.

Paul's children were already gathered around him. The rabbi stood at the end of the bed while Patricia and I sat on a nearby couch. After a little small talk with family, and a whispered conversation with Paul, the rabbi sang ancient Hebraic words in a deep baritone voice that penetrated the invisible barriers between Divinity and man.

Although I never asked what the words meant, we felt like pilgrims upon the great trail of life, our feet covered with a common dust. I could almost imagine the desert heat, the surrounding hills, the burning sun, the trailing shadow, the water now dispersed as song, quenching our thirst.

All signs of agitation drained from Paul's face.

"We all come from the same place, don't we?" Patricia asked when we returned to the upstairs living room.

"I think so."

"Oh, he loved to sing," she said. "If I'd known the rabbi would sing, I would have called him earlier."

A few days later, I received a phone call from one of our hospice volunteers. We'd met during a course I'd taught about spiritual presence. She called to say thank you, when she learned I'd visited Paul and Patricia.

"I don't have words for the healing around Paul's bedside," I said. "I'm not sure if it was the words or the resonance of the rabbi's voice, but it seemed to slip beneath scars and masks to reveal something we all share. I felt part of history, of humankind, of anything we might call Divine."

"Paul was a cantor, not only a singer. He deserved the best," she replied.

"I went to a Passover Seder once. It's the only other time I've heard such a depth of sound, as though all time stopped, and everything and everyone was holy.

"We were drunk on life, on food, on wine, one another, and something pure moved through every single word, disregarding any notion of belief in favor of gratitude."

She asked me for details, and as I recalled the date and location, she exclaimed, "Oh my God! My husband was the chef at that restaurant. It's the only Passover Seder ever offered there. He cooked for you and your friends. Paul was the cantor that night.

"You just sat vigil with the same man who once sang you through Passover."

We both marveled at the perfection.

"Maybe it's always been this simple," I wondered aloud. "We break bread. Drink wine. Sit with one another around the table and slip into the song that sings us all."

"May be," she replied. "May it be so."

EPILOGUE

AS I WRITE, FALL WHISPERS the portending tales of winter. The flowers seem to bow their heads in prayer each night as they slowly tuck petals, stamens, stems, and leaves back into the soil once more. Deciduous and evergreen trees bend into sculptures. Bees and wasps fight over the last drops of nectar then return home to ready their nests for winter.

Watching all the activity, I can't help but imagine the infinite number of stories reflected in any plot of land. There are more than any one of us could count in a lifetime.

Perhaps this is the real beauty—whatever we might call life, our life, has been part of this garden all along. To glimpse this, even once, is to know ourselves as flowers sharing the same ground of being.

From this view, the duality of good and bad falls away. We embrace this story, this life, as a unique reflection of a wholeness so vast we must lose ourselves to know it.

Death, and for that matter grief, are mirrors that point to this profundity as often as the necessity for change. This is true for all of us, without exception.

In this light, I ask that any reader approach the stories in this book as an invitation into the beauty rather than a guidebook against which to evaluate the fragile contours of living.

We do not need to compare one story against another, one life against another—we only need to listen. This is the love that can open even the most guarded heart.

As Paul said to the Corinthians, "Love never fails," even though, as the Dalai Lama said, "It might take a little longer."

Perhaps patience is another face of beauty—a constancy born from our willingness to show up for our neighbors, our enemies, and even the fragmented vulnerabilities lodged deep within us, begging for one small transformative moment of kindness.

Perhaps this has always been the journey—to open until nothing but the radiance of love remains.

May we be kind to one another, and to ourselves, in life and death.

ACKNOWLEDGMENTS

NO ONE CARES FOR the dying in isolation—a midwife is born within the arms of community. We give within a matrix of friends, colleagues, and family.

Although I represent one view of the dying process, the practice of spiritual care I offered was cultivated and supported within a professional milieu that offered me the freedom to serve our clientele at a time in history when most chaplains struggled to receive permission to make home visits at all.

In this, I thank Sarah, one of the grandmothers of hospice, who had the foresight to focus upon the potency of team work, and to hire someone outside of the box like me, and to Pam for having the administrative mastery and dedication to enact such a vision with unprecedented equality between professionals. I thank Mark for his wise counsel and far-reaching curiosity in the search for meeting the holistic needs of each client—your support showed me the true nature of leadership.

I thank the nurses who invited me to the bedside and trusted my medicine as readily as their own—I could not have had any success without your skills, humor, and utter commitment to the wellbeing of all. May everyone receive such openhearted medicine in their time of need.

I am also grateful to all the social workers who encouraged patients and their families to receive me. You wove a matrix of familial and social support so skillfully that even dire circumstances could look like home under your watchful eye. Your work enabled all of us to give what we had to give.

Thank you to all the home health aides for teaching me the true heart of spiritual care. You taught me the courage to greet the wholeness of being with openness, forgiveness, and kindness, knowing this is where we find anything we seek.

I also thank my fellow chaplains, spiritual caregivers, and spiritual midwives to the dying for your collegiality, your depth of questions, and your love for wisdom and human beings alike. Thank you for our conversations, the depths of your experience, the breadth of your intimacy with anyone you meet, your openness to the unknown as well as the dialogue, and for insisting I become a better person.

Thank you to all the volunteers who received spiritual teachings in a medical milieu and then walked into the homes of strangers with innocent eyes. You taught me that the capacity to be spiritually present to one another is a birthright, not a specialty.

I also thank all the ministers, priests, and spiritual care givers in my communities, with whom we shared the inquiry of care for our shared families. Most especially, I thank Janet for seeing me. You and your community taught me how to grow the seeds of wisdom hovering within my heart.

I also offer thanks to all the friends and students whoever attended a talk, class, or workshop and fearlessly asked questions that demanded real answers. You pushed me to find words for the wordless and to trust the solitude of presence when words failed. I am blessed within our endless circle of giving and receiving.

Finally, I wish to thank all the men and women who invited me into their homes—I prostrate in *namaste*. Although I have changed your names and any other identifying information, so your lives remain private, your sparks of soulness still dance in my heart as a revelation of the perfection life is. I pray I have honored a few of your gifts with this small book.

My personal life is a rich panoply of benevolence, so much so that it is impossible to say thank you to the seemingly infinite moments of kindness that led me here. I can only offer a small glimpse in these pages.

I want to thank my parents for including my brother and I in family ritual, hospital visits and conversations about illness and death in an era when most of my friends were sequestered from the truth. I learned how to laugh and cry on the same day and look into the face of fear even while trembling.

I thank my extended family, most especially Goldie and her sisters, for teaching me the magic of women around the kitchen table telling stories, the power of a good meal, and the simplicity of family helping family, of neighbor helping neighbor.

I thank a host of friends over the years, both new and old—Michelle, Pat, Susanna, Tina, Cindy, Cathleen, Nora, Gloria, Chris, Judy, Theresa, Tim, Laura D., Josh, Jill, Sean G., Josie, Randy, Jenny, Eric, Gwen, Lily, Susan, Joseph, Laura R., Peggy, Wendy, Tenzin, Sean A., Larry, Jan, Bill, Michael R., Jeffri, Joan, Dianne, Michael P., Lama Yeshe, Jennifer, Shannon, and Rebekha. It's true that we are the company we keep.

I thank Deana for standing in all those forks in the road with me and skillfully pointing me toward the light of dharma, teachers, and medicine, even when I could see nothing but the formless void. Thank you for introducing me to lineage.

I thank Sallie for being a beacon of all sangha everywhere and the bearer of kindness as I traversed the wilderness of retreat.

How precious to share these years with you, dear sister.

Finally, I am eternally grateful to all the sponsors who tirelessly supported me through my retreat. I still feel your prayerful presence each morning.

I am also blessed with teachers who taught from direct experience, not mere academic training. More often than not, their lives were the teachings, long before I understood their words.

I thank Alicia Cook and Kevin Oltjenbruns for having both the commitment and the courage to bring death, dying and grief coursework to the university environment, and for your prescient mentorship. May this small book honor your lifetimes of paving the way for the rest of us.

I thank Richard Groves and his Sacred Art of Living and Dying program. This comprehensive training in spiritual pain, cross-cultural views of death, and coma therapy became precious seeds that taught me how to think, listen, and offer spiritual care to the dying.

I thank Tari for teaching me how to dream the dream so deeply that I wanted to wake up. I would have had no gifts to give to the dying without those shared years. Any wisdom I discovered in retreat stood upon the meditative stability and psychological openness I first learned from you.

I also bow in gratitude to Lama Drimed Norbu. Here we are—isn't that something? May my life honor the lineage of teachings you are.

It's taken twelve years to bring this book to fruition if I include the years of service and the years of retreat required to distill all the gifts into something worth offering. Yet there were key people along the way.

I thank Chagdud Khadro, for asking me to tell a story from my work, and when I did, asked me to collect all my stories and write them down as an offering to others. My life pivoted upon this request. May this small offering honor all you give around the world.

I thank Bob and Tina for always following your visions and for including me within your network of family. This book has arisen from around your holiday tables as surely as my own heart. Thank you for helping me both clarify and manifest my own deep knowing of soul. Look, I did it!

I also thank Joe, my fearless protector and unrecognized Zen priest with a stick—I would not be here without your kindness. Who knows what heap of quitting these stories would have composted upon without your worldly skills, your unwavering trust, and your reckless altruism. Thank you from my deepest being. May you taste all you seek in the marrow of your own heart-mind.

I thank the Bolgia book group for bringing the private love of books into the intimacy of inquiry. You taught me the power of words and friendship. What was that saying about Vegas?

As this book wound its way to the public I found myself surrounded by gifted professionals and friends.

I thank Lama Drimed for pouring over the content of each story introduction, even offering last minute teachings to ensure I spoke with the highest integrity and wisdom I am capable of speaking. Any mistakes that might remain, are mine alone.

I thank Candace for her midwifery of words and for guiding me through the editing process in such a way that I could find my voice and carve sentences out of a desire to communicate rather than a fear of grammar. Thank you for holding the bigger picture as I grew into it.

I thank Dan and Gina for slipping past the inevitability of human profanity into the creative wonder of the heart. Thank you for trusting the process and for greeting this project with sincerity.

I thank Bodhi for forging an artistic and practical means to communicate with the world and patiently teaching me how my computer software works.

I thank Laurel for her generous contribution to The Mandorla Project. May this merit multiply and heal a multitude of beings, including the lingering questions of your soul.

Finally, I wish to thank Rob and Zach. Perhaps in another time or another place we could have forged all these trails together. For all the ways I thwarted this possibility, I am sorry. The losses we shared together were the earliest imprints of all that followed, but so was the love.

Rob, thank you for your unmitigated forgiveness and all the ways you maintained connection, even when you didn't have to. May you live the fullness of your deepest desires and know this to be the journey of your soul.

Zach, thank you for being who you are. It is a privilege to be your mother. I am grateful every day. You are a most precious human being. May you know this always.

I cannot finish my list of gratitude, without also thanking the high deserts, mountains, islands and sloughs upon which I have walked, learned, lived and served. I bow to the seen, and unseen, elemental wonders of our precious earth.

May all be filled with love, joy and abundance, with the freedom to pass it along.

NOTES

1 Joseph Campbell, *Pathways to Bliss: Mythology and Personal Transformation* (Novato, CA: New World Library, 2004), 7.

2 Frank Newport, "Most Americans Still Believe in God," *Social & Policy Issues,* June 29, 2016. Retrieved from https://news.gallup.com/poll/193271/americans-believe-god.aspx.

3 Joseph Campbell (2004), 7.

4 Joseph Campbell (2004), 4-10.

5 Joseph Campbell (2004), *xxv.*

6 David Whyte, *Consolations: The Solace, Nourishment and Underlying Meaning of Everyday Words* (Langley, WA: Many Rivers Press, 2014), 19.

7 Natasa Milicevic, "The Hospice Movement: History and current worldwide situation," *Archive of Oncology* 10:1 (2002): 29-32.

8 Richard Groves and Henriette Anne Klauser, *The American Book of Dying: Lessons in Healing Spiritual Pain* (Berkeley, CA: Celestial Arts, 2005), 13.

9 Hildegard of Bingen, Retrieved from https://quotefancy.com/quote/1569602/Hildegard-of-Bingen-What-I-do-not-see-I-do-not-know-I-see-hear-and-know-simultaneously.

10 Lama Drimed Norbu, Private Conversation, (2018).

11 Neil Douglas-Klotz, *The Sufi Book of Life: 99 Pathways of the Heart for the Modern Dervish* (New York, New York: Penguin Compass, 2005), 233.

12 David Whyte (2014), 39.

13 Psalm 121, trans. Stephen Mitchell, *A Book of Psalms: Selected and Adapted from the Hebrew* (New York, New York: HarperCollins Publishers, 1993), 67.

14 Psalm 121, trans. Stephen Mitchell (1993), 67.

15 Sister Chan Khong, *Learning True Love: Practicing Buddhism in a Time of War,* (Berkeley, CA: Parallax Press, 2007), 105-106.

16 Rene Descartes, *Discourse on the Method of Rightly Conducting the Reason and Seeking Truth in the Sciences,* (1637) Retrieved from http://newlearningonline.com/new-learning/chapter-7/descartes-i-think-therefore-i-am.

17 Stan Tomandl, *Coma Work and Palliative Care: An Introductory Communication Skills Manual for Supporting People Living Near Death* (Victoria, B.C.: White Bear Books, 1991).

18 Neil Douglas-Klotz, *Prayers of the Cosmos: Meditations on the Aramaic words of Jesus* (New York, New York: HarperSanFrancisco, 1990), 1-2.

19 Neil Douglas-Klotz (1990), 1-3.

20 Jane Hirshfield, *Nine Gates: Entering the Mind of Poetry* (New York, New York: Harper Perennial, 1997), *vii*.

21 Neil Douglas-Klotz, *Hidden Gospel: Decoding the Spiritual Message of the Aramaic Jesus* (Wheaton, Illinois: Quest Books, 1999), 57.

22 Rev. Brad Deford and Rev. Susan Cutshall, "Sharing the Mystery: Teaching Spiritual Care in Hospice," National Hospice Conference (Las Vegas, NV), 2004.

23 Chagdud Tulku Rinpoche, (9-15-2012), Retrieved from www.quotes.just-dharma.com.

24 Lama Drimed Norbu (2016) Private Conversation.

25 Chogyam Trungpa Rinpoche, *Crazy Wisdom* (Boston, MA: Shambhala Publications, 2001), 138.

26 David Whyte (2014), 118.

27 Rachel Naomi Remen, M.D., *Kitchen Table Wisdom: Stories That Heal* (New York: Riverhead Books, 1996), 3.

28 David Whyte (2014),46-48.

29 Ruth Ozeki, *A Tale for the Time Being* (New York, New York: Penguin Books, 2013), 364.

30 Zach Pike-Urlacher (2018) Private conversation.

31 John O'Donohue, *Anam Cara: A Book of Celtic Wisdom* (New York, New York: Harper Collins Publishers, 1997), *xviii*.

32 Lama Chönyi Zangmo (2011) Private Conversation.

33 1 Corinthians 13: 4-8, Revised Standard.

34 Neil Douglas-Klotz (2005), 216.

35 David Whyte (2014), 89-91.

36 Lorin Roche, *The Radiance Sutras: 112 Tantra Yoga Teachings for Opening to the Divine in Everyday Life*, Portable Edition (Marina del Rey, CA: Syzygy Creations, Inc., 2008), 37.

37 Lorin Roche (2008), 35.

38 Thomas Merton, *No Man is an Island* (New York, New York: Dell Publishing Company, Inc., 1955), 61.

ABOUT THE AUTHOR

AMITA LHAMO holds a Bachelor's degree in Human Development and Family Studies, and a Master's Degree in Marriage and Family Therapy. As a psychotherapist, she specialized in death, dying and grief, as well as trauma, chronic illness, and women's issues. As a spiritual practitioner, she has studied within the Lakota dream tradition, working with her first teacher for nearly a decade, before meeting the lineage of Chagdud Tulku Rinpoche, and studying with his Dzogchen lineage holder, Lama Drimed Norbu. Under his guidance, she completed a formal five-year meditation retreat in the Tibetan Buddhist tradition. She has cared for thousands of individuals and their families through the process of dying, both as a hospice chaplain, and as an independent midwife in her community. She was the spiritual care manager for Napa Valley Hospice and Adult Day Center, and has since trained individuals, groups, and organizations in spiritual care to the dying. She integrates her professional experience with her spiritual training to write and teach.

THE MANDORLA PROJECT

DEATH IS AN INEVITABLE part of life, yet it is also a necessary part of the spiritual path.

We at The Mandorla Project, a 501(c) organization, are dedicated to exploring the relationship between spirituality and care for the dying. We seek to cultivate and disseminate wisdom that can support professionals, caregivers, spiritual practitioners, and the dying, at any stage of life.

As we listen to the intelligence inherent in our spiritual traditions, as well as the heritages of our familial, communal, healing and medical traditions, we develop new ways to cultivate kindness.

We learn how to greet one another, honoring our unique differences, while embracing the essences we all share.

We began our imprint, Mandorla Publications, as a means to impart such wisdom in multi-media forms. *Dandelions Blooming in the Cracks of Sidewalks*, by Amita Lhamo, is our first offering.

For more information about our activities, visit our website at *www.themandorlaproject.org.*